Common Sense
Prescriptions For
Financial Health

Common Sense Prescriptions For Financial Health

Improving Your Quaestrology

Marvin H. Doniger

COMMON SENSE PRESCRIPTIONS FOR FINANCIAL HEALTH
IMPROVING YOUR QUAESTROLOGY

Copyright © 2011 by Marvin H. Doniger.

Library of Congress Control Number:		2011900849
ISBN:	Hardcover	978-1-4568-5483-6
	Softcover	978-1-4568-5482-9
	Ebook	978-1-4568-5484-3

Because of the dynamic nature of the Internet, any Web addresses or links contained in this book may have changed since publication and may no longer be valid.

The information, ideas, and suggestions in this book are not intended to render professional advice. Before following any suggestions contained in this book, you should consult your personal accountant or other financial advisor. Neither the author nor the publisher shall be liable or responsible for any loss or damage allegedly arising as a consequence of your use or application of any information or suggestions in this book.

This book was printed in the United States of America.

To order additional copies of this book, contact:
Xlibris Corporation
1-888-795-4274
www.Xlibris.com
Orders@Xlibris.com
91873

CONTENTS

CONSUMER UNIT PROFILES

In order to be able to evaluate the state of our quaestrology, there must be a reference point against which comparisons can be made. Fortunately, the Bureau of Labor Statistics has developed such a reference point. It is the consumer unit that consists of all the members of a given household. These consumer units (households) have been segmented by age and income groupings. In addition, there are data based on homeowners versus renters and region of the country in which the consumer units reside. As one might expect, the characteristics of these consumer units change with income and age.

As one leaves the cocoon of his/her parents, one must assume many of the financial obligations that were provided for him/her. One must obtain a means of transportation, shelter, clothing, and housing. After this initial solo flight into the outside world, most people form a bond with others and proceed to expand the size of their consumer unit. With the expansion of the consumer unit comes additional financial obligations. Ideally, income increases so as to satisfy these ever-increasing financial obligations. Ultimately, as one grows older, the size of the consumer unit decreases and so do the associated expenses. While physical health does deteriorate as we age, our financial health can, with careful planning, actually improve with age. If one has managed his/her finances, retirement can become the *golden years* not the *pyrite years.*

Those who are under twenty-five years have typically completed their education and have entered the workforce for the first time. Many of them will be burdened with education loans that they must start to repay. Their income typically should determine their lifestyle. Decisions that are made at this stage can have profound implications on their financial health. Some will seek housing and transportation that is affordable given their income. They should not indulge themselves with expensive clothing, gourmet foods, and lavish vacations. They should also start establishing a safety net for unexpected expenses and potential time without income. In addition, this is the optimal time in their lives to start saving for retirement. The longer the investment-time horizon, in this case forty-plus years, the higher is the probability of meeting one's financial goals. Those who incur financial obligations beyond their income risk a lifetime of precarious financial health. Unsupportable spending is akin to smoking and excessive consumption of food and alcohol. Coupling this with a sedentary lifestyle can almost guarantee a shortened life span.

By the time the head of consumer unit is forty-four years, most consumer units have been formed and have reached their ultimate size. There are children to be raised and educated that, in many cases, will require obtaining loans for higher education in cases where there are not adequate savings. Housing that was adequate before often must be replaced in order to accommodate the increased size of the consumer unit. Expenditures for food and clothing have increased as well. At this time, careers of the consumer-unit earners have been established and incomes have increased commensurate with their increased professional responsibilities. It is also at this time that unemployment may affect one or more earners within the consumer unit. Those with obsolete skills may find the job search lengthy and difficult. Progress against retirement goals must be evaluated and changes made where required. Consideration should be given to life insurance and disability insurance to protect the consumer unit should one or more earners become incapacitated.

As the head of the consumer unit approaches sixty-four years, the size of the consumer unit has changed as well as its demographics. Most children have reached adulthood and have formed their own households. Costs associated with raising and educating the children are behind and retirement looms on the horizon. It is also at this age where the earners in the consumer unit are most vulnerable to a loss of income either to illness, which might precipitate premature retirement, or through a loss of job that might not be able to be replaced. At this age, employers are very reluctant to hire someone despite the legal prohibitions against age discrimination. Insurance needs should be reevaluated and long-term care insurance should be considered.

When the head of consumer unit is older than sixty-five, the children have left the nest along with expenditures associated with providing for them. Those who have not adequately saved and invested for this time in their lives will certainly be living the *pyrite life* while those who have planned for this time in their lives can be living the *golden life*. Expenditures on housing and raising a family are replaced by increased health care costs and indulgences such as travel and other forms of recreation and entertainment. Spoiling grandchildren is often a favorite pastime during this period.

Profiles by Age of Head of Consumer Unit

From 1984 to 2008, consumer unit size, irrespective of its earnings, decreased by 3.8 percent, from 2.6 to 2.5 members. This reduction occurred in the less than eighteen years age group, which went from 0.7 to 0.6. The eighteen to sixty-four years and the sixty-four years and above were at the same level in 2008 as they were in 1984, 1.6 and 0.3 respectively. The size of consumer units whose head was less than twenty-five years increased from 1.8 in 1984 to 2.0 in 2008, an increase of 11.1 percent. This increase occurred in the eighteen to sixty-four year age group that went from 1.4 to 1.6. The size of consumer units whose head was between twenty-five and forty-four years remained constant at 3.1 people. In these consumer units, the number of members less than eighteen years decreased from 1.3 to 1.2 while those between eighteen and sixty-four years increased from 1.8 to 1.9. There were no members over sixty-four years in these consumer units. The size of consumer units whose head was in the forty-five to sixty-four-year age group decreased by 0.4 from 2.8 in 1984 to 2.4 in 2008. In these consumer units, the number of members less than eighteen years decreased from 0.5 to 0.4; between eighteen and sixty-four years from 2.2 to 2.0; and those over sixty-four years from 0.1 to less than 0.05. Finally, in those consumer units headed by someone over sixty-four years, their size and age composition was essentially the same in 2008 as it was in 1984.

	Consumer Unit Size by Age of Head of Consumer Unit (1984–2008)														
	Age of Head of Consumer unit														
	All			<25			25–44			45–64			64+		
	<18	18-64	64+	<18	18-64	64+	<18	18-64	64+	<18	18-64	64+	<18	18-64	64+
1984	0.7	1.6	0.3	0.4	1.4	0.0	1.3	1.8	0.0	0.5	2.2	0.1	0.1	0.3	1.4
1985	0.7	1.6	0.3	0.4	1.4	0.0	1.2	1.8	0.0	0.4	2.2	0.1	0.1	0.4	1.4
1986	0.7	1.6	0.3	0.4	1.4	0.0	1.3	1.8	0.0	0.4	2.2	0.1	0.1	0.4	1.3
1987	0.7	1.6	0.3	0.4	1.4	0.0	1.3	1.8	0.0	0.4	2.2	0.0	0.1	0.4	1.3
1988	0.7	1.6	0.3	0.4	1.4	0.0	1.2	1.8	0.0	0.4	2.1	0.0	0.1	0.3	1.4
1989	0.7	1.6	0.3	0.4	1.4	0.0	1.2	1.7	0.0	0.5	2.2	0.0	0.1	0.3	1.4
1990	0.7	1.6	0.3	0.4	1.4	0.0	1.2	1.8	0.0	0.4	2.2	0.0	0.1	0.4	1.4
1991	0.7	1.6	0.3	0.4	1.4	0.0	1.2	1.9	0.0	0.5	2.2	0.0	0.1	0.3	1.4
1992	0.7	1.5	0.3	0.4	1.5	0.0	1.2	1.8	0.0	0.4	2.2	0.0	0.1	0.3	1.4
1993	0.7	1.5	0.3	0.5	1.4	0.0	1.3	1.8	0.0	0.4	2.1	0.0	0.1	0.3	1.4
1994	0.7	1.5	0.3	0.5	1.5	0.0	1.3	1.8	0.0	0.4	2.1	0.0	0.1	0.3	1.4
1995	0.7	1.5	0.3	0.4	1.5	0.0	1.2	1.8	0.0	0.4	2.1	0.0	0.1	0.3	1.4
1996	0.7	1.5	0.3	0.4	1.4	0.0	1.2	1.8	0.0	0.4	2.1	0.0	0.1	0.3	1.4
1997	0.7	1.5	0.3	0.4	1.4	0.0	1.2	1.8	0.0	0.4	2.0	0.0	-0.8	1.2	1.3
1998	0.7	1.5	0.3	0.4	1.4	0.0	1.3	1.8	0.0	0.4	2.0	0.0	0.1	0.3	1.4
1999	0.7	1.5	0.3	0.4	1.4	0.0	1.2	1.9	0.0	0.4	2.0	0.0	0.1	0.3	1.4
2000	0.7	1.5	0.3	0.4	1.5	0.0	1.2	1.9	0.0	0.4	2.0	0.0	0.1	0.3	1.4
2001	0.7	1.5	0.3	0.3	1.6	0.0	1.3	1.9	0.0	0.4	2.0	0.0	0.1	0.3	1.4
2002	0.7	1.5	0.3	0.4	1.5	0.0	1.2	1.9	0.0	0.4	2.0	0.0	0.1	0.3	1.4
2003	0.6	1.6	0.3	0.4	1.4	0.0	1.2	1.9	0.0	0.4	1.9	0.0	0.1	0.3	1.4
2004	0.6	1.6	0.3	0.4	1.5	0.0	1.2	1.9	0.0	0.4	2.0	0.0	0.0	0.3	1.3
2005	0.6	1.6	0.3	0.5	1.6	0.0	1.2	1.8	0.0	0.4	2.0	0.0	0.1	0.3	1.4
2006	0.6	1.6	0.3	0.4	1.6	0.0	1.2	1.9	0.0	0.4	2.0	0.0	0.1	0.3	1.4
2007	0.6	1.6	0.3	0.4	1.6	0.0	1.2	1.8	0.0	0.4	2.0	0.0	0.1	0.3	1.4
2008	0.6	1.6	0.3	0.4	1.6	0.0	1.2	1.9	0.0	0.4	2.0	0.0	0.1	0.3	1.4

Table 2-1 Trends in consumer unit size based on age of head of consumer unit 1984–2008

Data *Bureau of Labor Statistics*

From 1984 to 2008, the average pretax annual income for all consumer units, irrespective of the age of their heads, increased from $23.5 thousand in 1984 to $63.6 thousand in 2008 for an average annual increase of 6.8 percent. It is of particular interest to observe that the average percentage annual increase in pretax income increased with the age of the head of the consumer unit. In consumer units whose head was less than twenty-five years, annual pretax income increased from $12.5 thousand to $28.1 thousand, an average annual increase of 5.0 percent. Consumer units whose head was between twenty-five and forty-four years consistently experienced the highest average annual pretax income. These consumer units had a 6.2 percent average annual increase in their pretax annual income, which went from $27.1 thousand to $69.3 thousand. In the case of consumer units headed by someone between forty-five and sixty-four years, annual pretax income increased from $28.4 thousand to $77.4 thousand, an average annual increase of 6.9 percent. Finally, in consumer units headed by someone sixty-four years and older, average annual pretax income increased at an average annual percentage rate of 7.1 from $14.1 thousand in 1984 to $39.3 thousand in 2008. It should be noted that the percentage increases in consumer units headed by someone less than twenty-five years, between forty-five to sixty-four years and over sixty-four years are distorted due to the lower base income against which percentage increases were calculated.

Consumer Unit Income by Age of Head of Consumer Unit (1984–2008)										
	Age of Head of Consumer unit					Age of Head of Consumer unit				
	All	<25	25–44	45–64	64+		All	<25	25–44	45–64	64+
1984	23.5	12.5	27.1	28.4	14.1	1997	39.9	15.7	45.0	50.0	23.9
1985	25.1	11.7	28.9	30.3	15.9	1998	41.6	16.8	46.8	53.1	23.9
1986	25.5	12.4	29.6	30.8	15.5	1999	44.0	18.3	48.7	55.7	26.6
1987	27.3	12.6	31.8	34.0	16.2	2000	44.6	19.7	51.7	54.7	25.1
1988	28.5	14.8	32.2	35.2	17.7	2001	47.5	20.8	54.8	57.5	27.5
1989	31.3	14.9	35.7	38.7	19.6	2002	49.4	20.8	56.1	60.2	29.6
1990	31.9	14.1	36.7	39.8	18.9	2003	51.1	20.7	56.3	64.1	30.4
1991	33.9	14.3	38.1	43.8	20.0	2004	54.5	22.8	59.7	66.4	35.0
1992	33.9	15.2	38.7	42.4	20.9	2005	58.7	27.5	64.7	70.5	36.9
1993	34.9	16.5	39.2	44.5	21.2	2006	60.5	29.1	67.2	71.6	38.0
1994	36.2	16.4	40.1	45.7	22.6	2007	63.1	31.4	67.5	76.4	40.3
1995	36.9	17.3	40.8	46.5	22.1	2008	63.6	28.1	69.3	77.4	39.3
1996	38.0	15.0	43.6	47.3	22.4						

Table 2-2   Trends in consumer unit based on pretax annual income (thousands) as a function of age of head of consumer unit

Data   *Bureau of Labor Statistics*

While the preceding increases in income are nice, it is interesting to examine the number of people in a consumer unit that was required to produce that income. The results are encouraging in that the number of earners required to support a consumer unit has, for the most part, remained the same or declined. With the exception of those whose head was between forty-five and sixty-four years, there was no net change in the number of earners in the consumer unit from 1984 to 2008. Those consumer units whose head was between forty-five and sixty-four years experienced a 10.1 percent reduction in the number of earners (1.7 to 1.5). The impact of the change in these consumer units produced a 7.1 percent decrease in the number of earners (1.4 to 1.3) in a consumer unit irrespective of the age of the head of consumer unit.

Earners per Consumer Unit by Age of Head of Consumer Unit (1984–2008)										
	Age of Head of Consumer Unit						Age of Head of Consumer Unit			
	All	<25	25–44	45–64	64+		All	<25	25–44	45–64	64+
1984	1.4	1.3	1.6	1.7	0.4	1997	1.3	1.2	1.6	1.6	0.4
1985	1.4	1.2	1.6	1.7	0.4	1998	1.3	1.2	1.6	1.6	0.4
1986	1.4	1.2	1.6	1.7	0.4	1999	1.3	1.3	1.6	1.6	0.4
1987	1.4	1.2	1.6	1.7	0.4	2000	1.4	1.3	1.6	1.6	0.4
1988	1.4	1.3	1.6	1.7	0.4	2001	1.4	1.3	1.6	1.6	0.5
1989	1.4	1.3	1.6	1.8	0.4	2002	1.4	1.3	1.6	1.6	0.5
1990	1.4	1.2	1.6	1.7	0.4	2003	1.3	1.2	1.6	1.6	0.4
1991	1.4	1.2	1.6	1.7	0.4	2004	1.3	1.3	1.6	1.5	0.4
1992	1.3	1.2	1.6	1.6	0.4	2005	1.3	1.4	1.6	1.5	0.5
1993	1.3	1.2	1.6	1.7	0.4	2006	1.3	1.3	1.6	1.5	0.5
1994	1.3	1.3	1.6	1.6	0.4	2007	1.3	1.3	1.6	1.6	0.5
1995	1.3	1.2	1.6	1.7	0.4	2008	1.3	1.3	1.6	1.5	0.4
1996	1.3	1.2	1.6	1.6	0.4						

Table 2-3   Trends in number of earners per consumer unit based on pretax annual income
Data   *Bureau of Labor Statistics*

Profiles by Consumer Unit Income

Since 1984, the number of people in consumer units with pretax annual income greater than $30.0 thousand declined from 3.2 to 2.7 in 2008, a decrease of 15.6 percent. The number of people under eighteen years declined by 20.1 percent from 0.9 to 0.7; the number between eighteen and sixty-five years decreased by 16.8 percent from 2.2 to 1.8; and the number over sixty-five years increased by over 100 percent from 0.1 to 0.2. In consumer units with annual pretax income between $30.0 thousand and $40.0 thousand, there was a 25.8 percent reduction in the number of members in those consumer units from 3.1 in 1984 to 2.3 in 2008, a 33.3 percent reduction in those younger than eighteen years and a 28.6 percent decrease in those between eighteen and sixty-five years. In these same consumer units the number of members older than sixty-five years increased from 0.1 to 0.2. Consumer units with pretax annual income between $40.0 thousand and $50.0 thousand experienced a 24.2 percent reduction in the number of its members (3.3 to 2.5). In these consumer units, the number of members under eighteen years decreased from 0.9 to 0.6, between eighteen and sixty-five years declined from 2.3 to 1.7 and over sixty-five years increased from 0.1 to 0.2. The number of members of consumer units with annual pretax income over $50.0 thousand declined from 3.3 to 3.0. In these consumer units, those under eighteen years declined from 0.9 to 0.8 and between eighteen and sixty-five years from 2.3 to 2.0. Those over sixty-five years increased from 0.1 to 0.2. This was the same increase that was observed in the other consumer units.

	ALL			$30–$40k			$40–$50k			>$50k		
	<18	18–65	>65	<18	18–65	>65	<18	18–65	>65	<18	18–65	>65
1984	0.9	2.2	0.1	0.9	2.1	0.1	0.9	2.3	0.1	0.9	2.3	0.1
1985	0.9	2.1	0.1	0.9	1.9	0.1	1.0	2.2	0.1	0.8	2.3	0.1
1986	0.9	2.1	0.2	0.9	1.9	0.2	1.0	2.0	0.2	0.8	2.2	0.2
1987	0.9	2.1	0.1	0.9	1.9	0.1	1.0	2.1	0.1	0.8	2.3	0.1
1988	0.9	2.0	0.1	0.9	1.9	0.1	1.0	2.1	0.1	0.8	2.2	0.1
1989	0.8	2.0	0.2	0.8	1.8	0.2	0.9	2.0	0.2	0.8	2.1	0.2
1990	0.9	2.0	0.1	0.8	1.9	0.1	0.9	2.0	0.1	0.9	2.2	0.1
1991	0.9	2.0	0.1	0.8	1.9	0.1	0.9	2.0	0.1	0.9	2.2	0.1
1992	0.8	2.0	0.2	0.8	1.7	0.2	0.9	1.9	0.2	0.9	2.1	0.2
1993	0.8	1.9	0.1	0.8	1.8	0.1	0.9	2.0	0.1	0.9	2.0	0.1
1994	0.8	2.0	0.1	0.8	1.8	0.1	0.9	1.9	0.1	0.9	2.1	0.1
1995	0.8	2.0	0.1	0.8	1.8	0.1	0.8	1.9	0.1	0.8	2.1	0.1
1996	0.9	1.9	0.2	0.8	1.7	0.2	0.8	1.9	0.2	0.9	2.0	0.2
1997	0.8	1.9	0.2	0.7	1.7	0.2	0.8	1.8	0.2	0.9	2.0	0.2
1998	0.8	1.9	0.2	0.7	1.6	0.2	0.8	1.7	0.2	0.9	2.0	0.2
1999	0.8	1.9	0.2	0.7	1.6	0.2	0.7	1.7	0.2	0.9	2.0	0.2
2000	0.8	1.9	0.2	0.7	1.6	0.2	0.7	1.7	0.2	0.9	2.1	0.2
2001	0.8	1.9	0.2	0.6	1.6	0.2	0.8	1.7	0.2	0.9	2.0	0.2
2002	0.8	1.9	0.2	0.6	1.7	0.2	0.7	1.7	0.2	0.9	1.9	0.2
2003	0.7	1.9	0.2	0.6	1.7	0.2	0.7	1.7	0.2	0.8	1.9	0.2
2004	0.7	1.9	0.2	0.6	1.6	0.2	0.7	1.7	0.2	0.8	2.0	0.2
2005	0.7	1.9	0.2	0.6	1.6	0.2	0.7	1.7	0.2	0.8	2.0	0.2
2006	0.7	1.8	0.2	0.6	1.5	0.2	0.6	1.7	0.2	0.8	1.9	0.2
2007	0.7	1.8	0.2	0.6	1.5	0.2	0.6	1.6	0.2	0.8	2.0	0.2
2008	0.7	1.8	0.2	0.6	1.5	0.2	0.6	1.7	0.2	0.8	2.0	0.2

Consumer Unit Size by Income Level
(1984–2008)

Table 2-4   Trends in consumer unit size based on pretax annual income over $30,000
Data   *Bureau of Labor Statistics*

During this same period, the age of the head of the consumer unit increased for those with annual pretax annual income of more than $30.0 thousand. It grew from 43.6 years in 1984 to 47.5 in 2008, an increase of 8.9 percent. The age of the head of consumer units with pretax annual income between $30.0 thousand and $40.0 thousand increased by 17.9 percent, from 41.9 years to 49.4 years. Those between $40.0 thousand and $50.0 thousand grew by 9.4 percent, from 43.8 years to 47.9 years and those greater than $50.0 thousand by 3.3 percent from 45.6 years to 47.1 years.

An interesting observation is the change in the age of consumer units with annual pretax income of between $30.0 thousand and $40.0 thousand as compared to the other income categories. From 1984 to 1990, this income group had the youngest head of a consumer unit. By 1991, the youngest head of a consumer unit was in the $40.0 thousand to $50.0 thousand annual pretax income group. By 1996, the age of consumer units with annual pretax income between $30.0 thousand and $40.0 thousand had the oldest head of consumer unit, 45.1 years. These changes are counterintuitive. One could reasonably expect the lowest income groups to have the youngest head of consumer unit not the oldest. It is beyond the scope of this book to understand the reasons for this phenomenon.

Age of Head of Consumer Unit by Income (1984–2008)								
	All	**$30–40K**	**$40–$50k**	**>$50k**		**All**	**$30–$40K**	**$40–$50k**	**>$50k**
1984	43.6	41.9	43.8	45.6	1997	44.9	45.1	44.4	44.9
1985	44.1	43.2	42.8	46.0	1998	44.7	45.3	44.2	44.7
1986	44.1	43.1	43.2	45.8	1999	45.1	45.8	44.7	45.0
1987	43.9	42.9	42.5	45.8	2000	45.1	46.3	44.7	44.8
1988	43.8	43.2	42.3	45.3	2001	45.6	46.8	45.3	45.2
1989	44.1	42.4	44.1	45.5	2002	46.0	47.7	46.4	45.4
1990	43.7	42.7	43.6	44.5	2003	46.3	47.4	46.7	45.9
1991	44.2	43.8	43.2	45.0	2004	46.8	47.5	47.3	46.6
1992	44.6	44.5	43.7	45.0	2005	46.7	47.9	46.8	46.4
1993	44.5	44.0	43.0	45.5	2006	46.9	48.2	47.5	46.5
1994	45.0	44.3	44.9	45.4	2007	47.2	48.6	46.8	46.9
1995	45.1	44.6	44.9	45.4	2008	47.5	49.4	47.9	47.1
1996	44.7	45.1	44.2	44.6					
Table 2-5 Data	Trends of age of head of consumer unit based on pretax annual income over $30,000 *Bureau of Labor Statistics*								

The number of people required to support consumer units with annual pretax income greater than $30.0 thousand declined from 0.65 in 1984 to 0.58 in 2008, a decrease of 10.8 percent. Those earning between $30.0 thousand and $40.0 thousand declined from 0.61 to 0.48, a decrease of 14.8 percent; between $40.0 and $50.0 thousand from 0.64 to 0.52, a decrease of 18.8 percent; and those greater than $50.0 thousand from 0.64 to 0.61, a decrease of 4.7 percent. As one might expect, the higher the annual pretax income of a consumer unit, the more members of the consumer unit had earned income. In 1984, consumer units with annual pretax income between $30.0 thousand and $40.0 thousand had 0.61 members who had earned income; between $40.0 thousand and

$50.0 thousand 0.64; and greater than $50.0 thousand 0.64. By 2008, the disparity between income groups had increased. There were 0.04 less income earners per consumer unit in the $30.0 thousand to $40.0 thousand group than in the $40.0 thousand to $50.0 thousand group (0.48 versus 0.52) and 0.13 less than in the greater than $50.0 thousand group (0.48 versus 0.61).

Earners per Consumer Unit by Income (1984–2008)								
	All	$30–40K	$40–$50k	>$50k		All	$30–$40K	$40–$50k	>$50k
1984	0.65	0.61	0.64	0.64	1997	0.63	0.58	0.61	0.66
1985	0.65	0.62	0.64	0.64	1998	0.63	0.56	0.59	0.66
1986	0.64	0.60	0.63	0.63	1999	0.64	0.56	0.62	0.67
1987	0.64	0.59	0.63	0.63	2000	0.62	0.56	0.58	0.64
1988	0.64	0.62	0.63	0.63	2001	0.63	0.58	0.59	0.66
1989	0.64	0.61	0.61	0.61	2002	0.61	0.52	0.58	0.64
1990	0.64	0.61	0.63	0.63	2003	0.61	0.52	0.58	0.65
1991	0.63	0.57	0.63	0.63	2004	0.60	0.54	0.54	0.63
1992	0.63	0.59	0.60	0.66	2005	0.60	0.50	0.54	0.63
1993	0.63	0.59	0.60	0.65	2006	0.61	0.52	0.56	0.64
1994	0.63	0.59	0.62	0.65	2007	0.60	0.48	0.54	0.63
1995	0.63	0.59	0.61	0.66	2008	0.58	0.48	0.52	0.61
1996	0.63	0.56	0.62	0.66	2009				

Table 2-6 Data — Trends in number of earners per consumer unit based on pretax annual income over $30,000
Bureau of Labor Statistics

Profiles by Housing Tenure

Stated simply, *housing tenure* is a term used to indicate whether a consumer unit owns its own residence or rents one. From 1984 to 2008, the size of a consumer unit that owned its home, irrespective of whether or not there was a mortgage on that home, declined by 10.3 percent from 2.9 to 2.6 people. Within that consumer unit, there was a 25.0 percent reduction in those under the age of eighteen years (0.8 to 0.6). During that same time period, the number of people between eighteen and sixty-five years decreased from 1.7 to 1.6, a 5.9 percent decline. The number of those over sixty-five years stayed constant at 0.4.

Unlike the case with homeowners, the size of consumer units that rented their homes was the same in 2008 as it was in 1984, 2.2 people. This should not be a surprise since an expanding family size is often a reason to buy a house rather than rent an apartment. In all age groups, the number of people in each age group, despite changes in particular years, ended where they started. The number of people under eighteen years at 0.6; between eighteen and sixty-five years at 1.4; and over sixty-five years at 0.2. As compared to consumer units who owned their home, the renters in 1984 had 0.2 less members under eighteen years (0.6 versus 0.8), 0.3 less between eighteen and sixty-five years (1.7 versus 1.4) and 0.2 less over sixty-five years (0.4 to 0.2). By 2008, the same number of members under eighteen existed within both groups (0.6). In addition, the difference in the number between eighteen and sixty-five years had become 0.2 people, (1.6 versus 1.4). There was no change in the differential among those over sixty-five years.

Consumer Unit Size by Housing Tenure (1984–2008)												
	Homeowner			Renter				Homeowner			Renter		
	<18	18–65	>65	<18	18–65	>65		<18	18–65	>65	<18	18–65	>65
1984	0.8	1.7	0.4	0.6	1.4	0.2	1997	0.7	1.6	0.4	0.7	1.4	0.1
1985	0.7	1.8	0.4	0.6	1.3	0.2	1998	0.7	1.6	0.4	0.6	1.5	0.1
1986	0.7	1.7	0.4	0.6	1.4	0.2	1999	0.7	1.5	0.4	0.7	1.4	0.2
1987	0.7	1.7	0.4	0.7	1.3	0.2	2000	0.7	1.5	0.4	0.7	1.4	0.2
1988	0.7	1.7	0.4	0.7	1.4	0.2	2001	0.7	1.5	0.4	0.6	1.4	0.2
1989	0.7	1.7	0.4	0.7	1.3	0.2	2002	0.7	1.5	0.4	0.6	1.5	0.1
1990	0.7	1.6	0.4	0.7	1.4	0.2	2003	0.7	1.5	0.4	0.6	1.5	0.1
1991	0.7	1.6	0.4	0.7	1.4	0.2	2004	0.7	1.5	0.4	0.6	1.5	0.1
1992	0.7	1.6	0.4	0.7	1.4	0.2	2005	0.6	1.6	0.4	0.6	1.4	0.2
1993	0.7	1.6	0.4	0.7	1.4	0.2	2006	0.6	1.6	0.4	0.6	1.4	0.2
1994	0.7	1.6	0.4	0.7	1.4	0.2	2007	0.6	1.6	0.4	0.6	1.4	0.2
1995	0.7	1.6	0.4	0.7	1.4	0.2	2008	0.6	1.6	0.4	0.6	1.4	0.2
1996	0.7	1.6	0.4	0.7	1.4	0.2							

Table 2-7   Trends in consumer unit size based on home ownership and renting.
Data   *Bureau of Labor Statistics*

As one would expect, the age of the head of consumer unit that owned its home was higher than in consumer units that rented one. In 1984, the age of a home-owning consumer unit was 51.1 years while in a renting consumer unit it was 39.3 years, a difference of 11.8 years. By 2008, their respective ages were 52.9 and 41.5 years, a difference of 11.4 years.

	All	Own	Rent		All	Own	Rent		All	Own	Rent
Age of Head of Consumer Unit by Housing Tenure (1984–2008)											
1984	46.7	51.1	39.3	1993	47.8	52.7	39.5	2002	48.1	52.0	40.4
1985	46.8	51.3	39.4	1994	47.6	52.2	39.8	2003	48.4	52.2	40.6
1986	46.7	51.4	39.1	1995	48.0	52.3	40.3	2004	48.5	52.3	40.4
1987	47.0	51.5	39.8	1996	47.7	52.2	39.8	2005	48.6	52.3	40.9
1988	47.0	51.6	39.5	1997	47.7	52.2	39.9	2006	48.7	52.2	41.5
1989	47.2	51.8	39.5	1998	47.6	52.1	39.6	2007	48.8	52.5	41.3
1990	47.2	51.9	39.3	1999	47.9	52.1	40.1	2008	49.1	52.9	41.5
1991	47.5	51.9	40.1	2000	48.2	52.3	40.3				
1992	47.6	52.4	40.0	2001	48.1	52.1	40.3				

Table 2-8 Trends in age of heads of consumer unit that were homeowners versus renters.
Data *Bureau of Labor Statistics*

When one considers all consumer units, irrespective of their housing tenure, the number of earners decreased from 1.4 in 1984 to 1.3 in 2008. During this same time period, the number of earners in a consumer unit that owned its home decreased from 1.5 to 1.4 while the number of earners in consumer units that rented increased from 1.1 to 1.2.

	All	Own	Rent		All	Own	Rent		All	Own	Rent
Earners per Consumer Unit Based on Tenure (1984–2008)											
1984	1.4	1.5	1.1	1993	1.3	1.4	1.1	2002	1.4	1.4	1.2
1985	1.4	1.5	1.1	1994	1.3	1.4	1.1	2003	1.3	1.4	1.2
1986	1.4	1.5	1.1	1995	1.3	1.5	1.1	2004	1.3	1.4	1.2
1987	1.4	1.5	1.2	1996	1.3	1.5	1.2	2005	1.3	1.4	1.2
1988	1.4	1.5	1.2	1997	1.3	1.4	1.2	2006	1.3	1.4	1.2
1989	1.4	1.5	1.2	1998	1.3	1.4	1.2	2007	1.3	1.4	1.2
1990	1.4	1.5	1.2	1999	1.3	1.4	1.2	2008	1.3	1.4	1.2
1991	1.4	1.5	1.2	2000	1.4	1.4	1.2				
1992	1.3	1.4	1.2	2001	1.4	1.4	1.2				

Table 2-9 Trends in number of earners per consumer unit that were homeowners versus renters.
Data *Bureau of Labor Statistics*

Profiles by Region

An analysis of the size of consumer units, irrespective of the region of the country in which they resided, from 1984 to 2008 reveals that the number of people decreased from 2.6 to 2.5 people. This reduction occurred in the under eighteen years category. In the Northeast, a decrease from 2.5 people to 2.4 occurred in the over sixty-five years, which went from 0.4 to 0.3 members. The Midwest remained the same with 0.8 members under eighteen years, 1.6 between eighteen and sixty-five years, and 0.3 over sixty-five years. The South declined from 2.7 to 2.5 people. The under eighteen years and the eighteen to sixty-five years group each lost 0.1 members, 0.7 to 0.6 and 1.7 to 1.6 respectively. The gain of 0.1 people in the West occurred in the eighteen to sixty-five years category, which went from 1.5 to 1.6. The under eighteen group was the same in 2008 as in 1984, 0.7 people and the over sixty-five years, 0.3 people.

Consumer Unit Size by Region
(1984–2008)

	All			Northeast			Midwest			South			West		
	<18	18–65	>65	<18	18–65	>65	<18	18–65	>65	<18	18–65	>65	<18	18–65	>65
1984	0.7	1.6	0.3	0.6	1.5	0.4	0.8	1.6	0.3	0.7	1.7	0.3	0.7	1.5	0.3
1985	0.7	1.6	0.3	0.6	1.5	0.3	0.7	1.6	0.3	0.7	1.7	0.3	0.7	1.6	0.3
1986	0.7	1.6	0.3	0.6	1.6	0.3	0.7	1.5	0.3	0.7	1.6	0.3	0.7	1.6	0.3
1987	0.7	1.6	0.3	0.6	1.5	0.4	0.7	1.5	0.3	0.7	1.6	0.3	0.7	1.6	0.3
1988	0.7	1.6	0.3	0.6	1.6	0.3	0.7	1.6	0.3	0.7	1.6	0.3	0.7	1.6	0.3
1989	0.7	1.6	0.3	0.6	1.6	0.3	0.7	1.6	0.3	0.7	1.6	0.3	0.7	1.6	0.3
1990	0.7	1.6	0.3	0.6	1.6	0.3	0.7	1.5	0.3	0.7	1.5	0.3	0.8	1.5	0.3
1991	0.7	1.6	0.3	0.6	1.6	0.3	0.7	1.5	0.3	0.7	1.5	0.3	0.8	1.6	0.3
1992	0.7	1.5	0.3	0.6	1.5	0.3	0.7	1.6	0.3	0.7	1.5	0.3	0.8	1.6	0.3
1993	0.7	1.5	0.3	0.6	1.5	0.4	0.7	1.5	0.3	0.7	1.5	0.3	0.8	1.6	0.3
1994	0.7	1.5	0.3	0.7	1.4	0.4	0.7	1.5	0.3	0.7	1.5	0.3	0.8	1.6	0.3
1995	0.7	1.5	0.3	0.6	1.5	0.4	0.7	1.5	0.3	0.7	1.5	0.3	0.8	1.6	0.3
1996	0.7	1.5	0.3	0.7	1.5	0.3	0.7	1.5	0.3	0.7	1.5	0.3	0.8	1.5	0.3
1997	0.7	1.5	0.3	0.6	1.6	0.3	0.7	1.5	0.3	0.7	1.5	0.3	0.8	1.6	0.3
1998	0.7	1.5	0.3	0.6	1.6	0.3	0.7	1.5	0.3	0.7	1.5	0.3	0.7	1.6	0.3
1999	0.7	1.5	0.3	0.6	1.6	0.3	0.7	1.5	0.3	0.7	1.5	0.3	0.7	1.6	0.3
2000	0.7	1.5	0.3	0.6	1.6	0.3	0.7	1.5	0.3	0.7	1.5	0.3	0.7	1.6	0.3
2001	0.7	1.5	0.3	0.6	1.6	0.3	0.6	1.5	0.3	0.7	1.5	0.3	0.7	1.6	0.3
2002	0.7	1.5	0.3	0.6	1.6	0.3	0.7	1.5	0.3	0.6	1.6	0.3	0.7	1.6	0.3
2003	0.6	1.6	0.3	0.6	1.5	0.3	0.6	1.6	0.3	0.6	1.6	0.3	0.7	1.6	0.3
2004	0.6	1.6	0.3	0.6	1.5	0.3	0.6	1.5	0.3	0.6	1.6	0.3	0.7	1.6	0.3
2005	0.6	1.6	0.3	0.6	1.5	0.3	0.6	1.5	0.3	0.6	1.6	0.3	0.7	1.6	0.3
2006	0.6	1.6	0.3	0.6	1.5	0.3	0.6	1.5	0.3	0.7	1.5	0.3	0.7	1.6	0.3
2007	0.6	1.6	0.3	0.6	1.5	0.3	0.6	1.5	0.3	0.7	1.5	0.3	0.7	1.6	0.3
2008	0.6	1.6	0.3	0.6	1.5	0.3	0.8	1.6	0.3	0.6	1.6	0.3	0.7	1.6	0.3

Table 2-10 Data Trends in consumer unit size based on region of country
Bureau of Labor Statistics

As one studies the income per consumer unit in the various regions, one cannot help but notice the wide disparities in consumer unit income between the various regions. An examination of the pretax annual income of all earners, including those earning less than $30.0 thousand, shows that it averaged $41.4 thousand as it increased from

$23.5 thousand in 1984 to $63.6 thousand in 2008, an annual average increase of 6.8 percent. In descending order, the average annual pretax income was highest in the Northeast at $44.6 thousand, followed by the West at $44.5 thousand, the Midwest at $40.1 thousand and the South with the lowest at $38.6 thousand. Their respective annual increases in pretax annual income were 7.6, 6.7, 6.9, and 6.4 percent.

	All	**Northeast**	**Midwest**	**South**	**West**		**All**	**Northeast**	**Midwest**	**South**	**West**
1984	23.5	24.2	22.4	22.7	25.4	**1997**	39.9	43.3	39.2	35.7	44.4
1985	25.1	25.4	24.1	24.7	26.9	**1998**	41.6	45.3	40.9	38.4	44.0
1986	25.5	26.6	23.3	24.6	28.6	**1999**	44.0	48.3	42.0	40.4	47.5
1987	27.3	27.5	25.8	26.5	30.4	**2000**	44.6	47.4	44.4	42.0	46.7
1988	28.5	29.8	27.4	27.3	30.6	**2001**	47.5	50.6	47.7	44.2	50.0
1989	31.3	34.1	29.5	29.7	33.4	**2002**	49.4	54.0	49.2	45.6	52.0
1990	31.9	35.5	29.0	29.6	35.4	**2003**	51.1	56.5	52.4	46.7	52.5
1991	33.9	37.0	31.5	31.7	37.2	**2004**	54.5	61.1	53.6	50.8	55.7
1992	33.9	36.9	32.2	31.0	37.2	**2005**	58.7	63.1	56.6	53.3	65.9
1993	34.9	37.5	33.6	32.4	37.6	**2006**	60.5	64.2	58.0	56.2	67.0
1994	36.2	39.1	33.5	33.7	40.2	**2007**	63.1	69.9	59.4	58.2	68.9
1995	36.9	39.5	36.4	33.8	39.9	**2008**	63.6	70.4	61.1	58.9	68.0
1996	38.0	40.6	38.0	35.6	39.8						

Income per Consumer Unit by Region
(1984–2008)

Table 2-11	Trends in pretax income (thousands) per consumer unit based on region of country.
Data	*Bureau of Labor Statistics*

From 1984 to 2008, the number of earners per consumer unit was relatively constant. The Northeast and South averaged 1.3 earners per consumer unit; the Midwest and West 1.4. In no year was the number of earners per consumer unit greater than 1.4 or less than 1.2.

| | | | Earners per Consumer Unit by Region | | | | | | | | |
| | | | (1984–2008) | | | | | | | | |
	All	Northeast	Midwest	South	West		All	Northeast	Midwest	South	West
1984	1.4	1.3	1.4	1.4	1.4	1997	1.3	1.3	1.4	1.3	1.4
1985	1.4	1.3	1.4	1.4	1.4	1998	1.3	1.3	1.4	1.3	1.4
1986	1.4	1.4	1.3	1.4	1.4	1999	1.3	1.4	1.4	1.3	1.4
1987	1.4	1.3	1.4	1.4	1.4	2000	1.4	1.3	1.4	1.3	1.4
1988	1.4	1.3	1.4	1.4	1.4	2001	1.4	1.3	1.4	1.3	1.4
1989	1.4	1.4	1.4	1.3	1.4	2002	1.4	1.3	1.4	1.3	1.4
1990	1.4	1.4	1.4	1.4	1.4	2003	1.3	1.3	1.4	1.3	1.4
1991	1.4	1.3	1.4	1.4	1.4	2004	1.3	1.3	1.4	1.3	1.4
1992	1.3	1.3	1.4	1.3	1.4	2005	1.3	1.3	1.4	1.3	1.4
1993	1.3	1.3	1.4	1.3	1.4	2006	1.3	1.3	1.4	1.3	1.4
1994	1.3	1.2	1.3	1.3	1.4	2007	1.3	1.3	1.4	1.3	1.4
1995	1.3	1.3	1.4	1.3	1.4	2008	1.3	1.3	1.3	1.3	1.4
1996	1.3	1.3	1.4	1.3	1.4	2009					

Table 2-12	Trends in number of earners per consumer unit based on region of country.
Data	*Bureau of Labor Statistics*

From 1984 to 2008, there was a steady increase in the age of the head of the consumer unit in all regions. In the aggregate, the age of the head of consumer unit increased at an average annual rate of 0.1 percent from 46.7 years in 1984 to 48.0 years in 2008. The Northeast had the highest average age of the head of a consumer unit at 48.5 years, followed by the Midwest at 47.4 years, the South at 47.2 years, and the West at 45.9 years. The Northeast, Midwest, and South had average annual increases in the age of the head of the consumer unit of 0.1 percent. In the West, the average increased 0.2 percent.

Age of Head of Consumer Unit by Region
(1984–2008)

	All	Northeast	Midwest	South	West		All	Northeast	Midwest	South	West
1984	46.7	48.6	47.1	46.2	44.7	1997	46.7	48.6	47.1	46.2	44.7
1985	46.8	47.7	47.7	46.6	44.8	1998	46.8	47.7	47.7	46.6	44.8
1986	46.7	47.8	47.2	46.1	46.1	1999	46.7	47.8	47.2	46.1	46.1
1987	47.0	49.1	46.9	46.6	45.8	2000	47.0	49.1	46.9	46.6	45.8
1988	47.0	48.6	46.9	47.1	45.2	2001	47.0	48.6	46.9	47.1	45.2
1989	47.2	48.6	46.9	47.4	45.8	2002	47.2	48.6	46.9	47.4	45.8
1990	47.2	48.0	46.9	47.7	45.7	2003	47.2	48.0	46.9	47.7	45.7
1991	47.5	48.7	47.1	47.6	46.7	2004	47.5	48.7	47.1	47.6	46.7
1992	47.6	48.3	47.7	47.8	46.5	2005	47.6	48.3	47.7	47.8	46.5
1993	47.8	49.0	47.9	47.7	46.7	2006	47.8	49.0	47.9	47.7	46.7
1994	47.6	49.4	47.5	47.5	46.4	2007	47.6	49.4	47.5	47.5	46.4
1995	48.0	49.4	48.0	47.9	46.7	2008	48.0	49.4	48.0	47.9	46.7
1996	47.7	48.1	48.8	47.7	46.1						

Table 2-13 Trends of the age of head of consumer unit that were homeowners versus renters.
Data *Bureau of Labor Statistics*

QUAESTROLOGY

Physiology, the study of the functions of the human body, is used by physicians to determine the physical health of their patients. Quaestrology, a holistic study of the financial issues affecting the individual, addresses the individual's financial obligations and the sources of income and assets that are available to service current as well as both planned and unforeseen needs. The medical profession has developed a set of vital signs with which the health of an individual can be determined. The accounting profession has developed measures of a company's financial condition. Quaestrology has also developed measures by which the individual's financial condition can be determined. Before examining these measures, it is important to understand how one's financial condition evolves as one progresses through life's stages. (For a further discussion of life's stages refer to *A Common Sense Road Map to Uncommon Wealth*).

During childhood (birth to twenty-one years of age), we progress from being totally dependent on our families to being independent and ideally self-sufficient. At birth, we are totally dependent on them for food, shelter, clothes, toys, etc. Many of the traits that will guide us in later life are developed during this stage of our lives. Of relevance to our quaestrology is our proclivity to spending versus saving. Those of us who spend more than we have will find it difficult to adjust our spending habits when we are on our own. Saving a portion of the monies we receive from allowances, birthdays, etc., is an excellent mechanism for introducing the concept of saving into our priorities. It is also during this period in our lives that we may incur significant financial obligations that must be repaid later in our lives. Investments in our education are financial obligations that those of us who are not fortunate enough to have had our parents pay for will have to be repaid by us. This kind of financial obligation is really an investment in ourselves and has been proven to significantly increase earnings over a lifetime. Credit card debt is an example of financial obligations that do nothing other than burden us with bills that must be repaid.

It is during young adulthood (ages twenty-one to forty-two) that we take responsibility for our careers and financial obligations. We assume some of the most significant obligations of our lives. Most of us marry, have children, purchase a home, and save for unexpected financial obligations as well as retirement. In addition, many of us will have car payments to make and education loans to repay. We must wisely make trade-offs between current consumption and investments in the future well-being of our family. In addition, we face potential financial crises due to loss of job, medical emergencies, or the need to provide assistance to our parents. What must be avoided are unnecessary financial obligations that cannot readily be repaid.

Middle age (ages forty-two to sixty-three) involves the recognition of our limitations and the refinement of our life's goals. It is at this juncture in our lives that we become more aware of the deterioration of our health. In fact, many of us may face our first serious illnesses. Some of us may be forced to retire or seek lower incomes as a result of deteriorating health or loss of job. For most of us, some of our financial obligations, such as raising our children, have been satisfied while others, such as providing for our retirement, still remain ahead of us. Whether we divert the financial resources we invested in our children to our retirement or to our current standard of living will be critical in determining the quality of life during our old age. What we do not want to do is incur frivolous, unaffordable financial obligations.

Old age can be golden years if we have lived a healthy lifestyle and prepared wisely for our retirement. This is the time when the decisions that we either consciously or subconsciously made can be evaluated. If we made good decisions, then we can reap the rewards of those decisions and the resulting sacrifices that we might have made. If our decisions were wrong, then we must suffer the consequences. The greater our existing financial obligations, the more savings we will need to see us through retirement. At this stage of our lives, it becomes virtually impossible to finance the remainder of our lives unless we had prepared previously in life. While some of us may be able to work at this point in our lives, most of us should not plan on being able to do so.

Despite the stage of life that we may be in, care should be taken to carefully define for ourselves what our basic needs are. While we all need food, shelter, and clothing, we should ensure that we define these basic needs such that we can afford them. At times in our lives, we may have to stretch beyond what we can afford for these items. However, we should not assume that we can do so forever. Beyond our basic needs, there are needs for safety. Just as we insure our automobiles, we should also consider protecting ourselves and our families from illness, disability, and death. In addition to safety needs, we should save for future needs such as purchasing a home, building an education fund for our children, and saving for our retirement. Once our basic and safety needs are satisfied, we can consider indulging ourselves. Just as with eating, we should not overindulge in what we buy. Instead of becoming obese by not controlling the relationship between the calories we consume and the calories we burn, we must maintain the proper balance between our income sources and our expenditures. While it is perfectly acceptable to occasionally splurge on a decadent dessert or piece of jewelry, dress, vacation, etc., a constant pattern of such excessive behavior can be detrimental to our financial physiology or quaestrology. In some cases, such as continual excessive splurging on expensive meals, we may damage our physical as well as financial well-being. Purchases that make us feel good should be made only after the financial consequences are understood. Each of us must distinguish between what we need and what we desire.

As depicted in the following chart, quaestrology comprises the flow of financial resources used to satisfy financial obligations. Earned income can be allocated between savings and satisfying financial obligations. Savings can be reinvested to accrue compound returns or be used to satisfy financial obligations. In addition, if earned income and savings are not sufficient to meet financial obligations, then borrowing might be required. The key to building wealth is managing earned income so as to be able to contribute to savings and satisfy financial obligations without liquidating savings or borrowing. Since most of us have limited ability to increase earned income in the short term, the key to having a healthy quaestrology is to control financial obligations. It is the financial obligations that we incur that are the critical element in our financial health.

The physician takes our physiological vital signs such as blood pressure, heart rate, temperature, etc., to determine our physical health. Our capacity to meet our financial obligations is the means by which we measure our fiscal health. Short-term obligations should be covered by earned income, medium-term obligations by earned income and savings, and long-term obligations by borrowings that can serviced by future current income. Just as high blood pressure is detrimental to our physical healthy, borrowing that is serviced by additional borrowing is detrimental to our financial health.

For most of us, our primary source of income will be what we are able to earn from our jobs. As we become more productive in our jobs, it is not unrealistic to expect our income to increase. In certain years, our incomes may increase more than in others due to circumstances beyond our control. During difficult economic conditions, employers are often unable to be as generous with their employees as in times of prosperity. In order to increase our earnings, it may become necessary to change professions, employers, or take on an additional job. In addition to the primary breadwinner, other members of the family may need to seek employment to cover short-term or longer-term financial obligations. In the ideal cases, one family member's income would be sufficient, and the other's could be either entirely or partially saved.

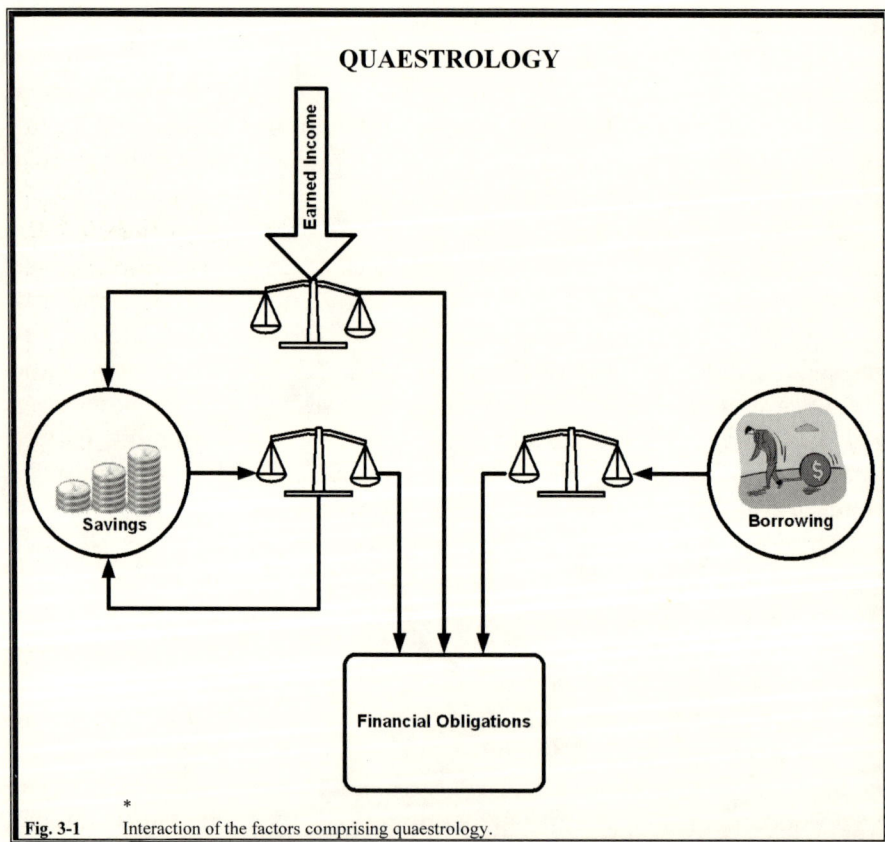

QUAESTROLOGY

Fig. 3-1   Interaction of the factors comprising quaestrology.

Consumer Income

It should be of no surprise that in 2008, wages and salaries accounted for 80.2 percent of consumer income before taxes. Social Security along with private and government retirement payments accounted for 10.3 percent; self-employment income 5.1 percent; interest, dividends, rental, and other property income 2.4 percent; and unemployment and workers' compensation, veterans' benefits, public assistance, supplemental security income, food stamps, support payments, and other miscellaneous income accounted for 2.0 percent. Obviously, very few, if any, consumers had all these sources of income. But for the population at large, these were its sources of income.

In the aggregate, the U.S. population in 2008 earned $63,563, paid taxes of $1,789, received $1,209 in gifts of goods and services, and owned a home whose value was estimated to be $169,794.

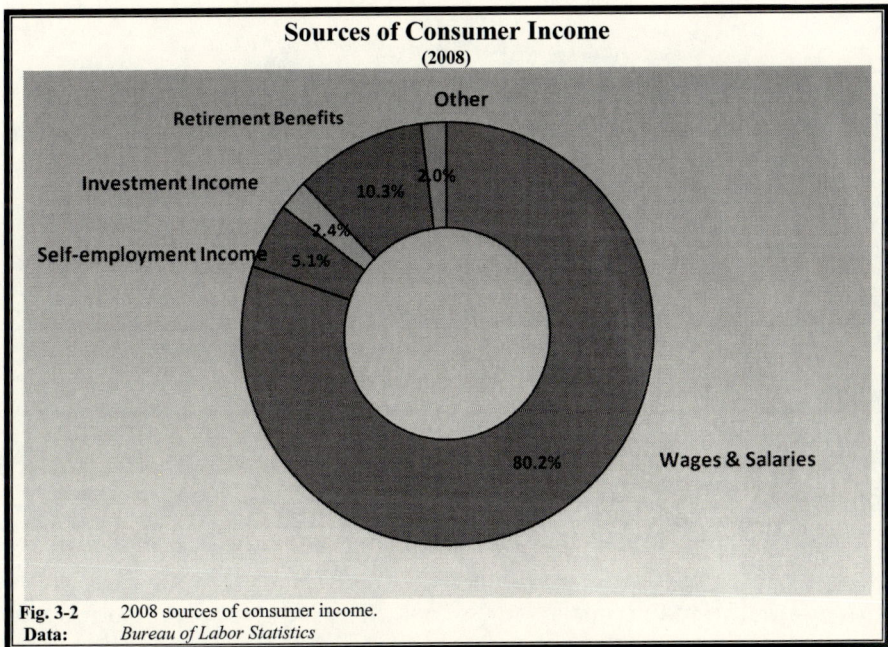

Sources of Consumer Income
(2008)

Other
Retirement Benefits
Investment Income   10.3%   2.0%
Self-employment Income   2.4%
                           5.1%
                                          80.2%   Wages & Salaries

Fig. 3-2   2008 sources of consumer income.
Data: *Bureau of Labor Statistics*

Consumer Expenditures

In addition to income and its sources, one must examine how consumers spend their money. As the following chart shows, housing-related expenses accounted for 27.7 percent of the average consumer's expenditures in 2008; transportation for 13.9 percent; food for 10.4 percent; personal insurance and pensions for 9.1 percent; other, which consists of personal care products, reading, education, tobacco products and smoking, cash contributions, alcoholic beverages and miscellaneous items, accounted for 8.3 percent; health care 4.8 percent; entertainment 4.6 percent; and apparel and services 2.9 percent. After accounting for all of these expenditures, the average consumer had 18.3 percent of his/her disposable income left over.

Distribution of Consumer Expenditures
(2008)

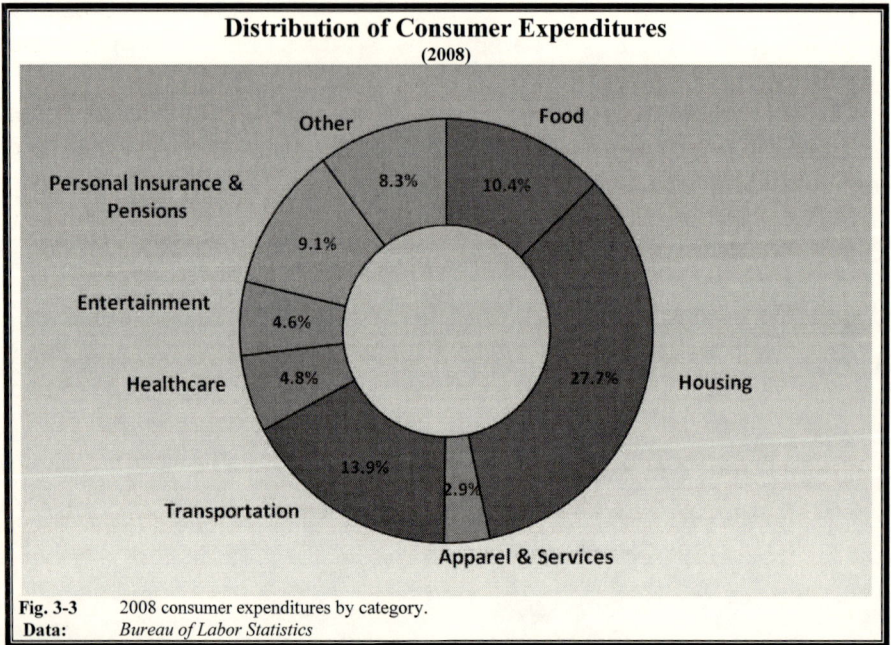

| Fig. 3-3 | 2008 consumer expenditures by category. |
| Data: | *Bureau of Labor Statistics* |

Consumer Income Statement

As stated previously, it is the relationship between our expenditures and our income that determines our financial well-being. The more money that remains after our expenditures have been subtracted from our disposable (after tax) income, the more secure our financial condition. The consumer income statement inventories the various sources of gross income as well as the various taxes and categories and subcategories of expenditures that result in our having a net positive (profit) or negative (loss) position during the time period covered by the income statement. The composition of the consumer unit greatly influences the sources of income and the expenditures upon which that income is spent. Younger consumer units have different expenses than older ones. Similarly, lower income consumer units have different expenses than wealthier ones; homeowners than renters; consumer units in the South than those in the East, Midwest, and West; and those in urban areas than in rural areas.

Gross income consists of wages and salaries, which is the primary source of income for most consumer units. In addition, some consumer units have other sources of income, such as self-employment income, social security and other retirement income, investment income, such as interest and dividends, public assistance, contributions from others, and benefits, such as unemployment, workers' compensation, and veterans' benefits.

Personal taxes must be subtracted from gross income in order to determine the income that is available for expenditures and savings. Personal taxes consist of federal income taxes, social security deductions, state and local income taxes, and any other taxes that are based on income. For most people, these personal taxes are such that there are few legal ways of avoiding them. However, it is how we use our disposable income that determines our quaestrology.

Perhaps the single most important factor that determines our financial health is how we choose to spend money. If we are prudent and live within our means, then we have a higher probability of financial well-being. On the other hand, if we continually live beyond our means, then our financial health is at risk. It is analogous to how diet and lifestyle affects our physical health. Those who smoke, drink excessively, eat unhealthy foods, and are sedentary assume higher risk of serious illnesses and a shortened life span. Those who continually live beyond their means surely risk financial insecurity.

Consumer obligations can be viewed as being fixed, variable, and discretionary obligations. Fixed obligations are ones whose size is a constant for a period of time irrespective of usage. Mortgage, car payments, and health insurance premiums are examples of fixed obligations. As opposed to fixed obligations, variable obligations are those whose size is influenced by usage. Examples of variable obligations are housing costs, such as utilities; transportation costs, such as gasoline, food; and health care costs, such as medical services and medicine. Discretionary obligations are those in which the consumer can forego or reduce without enduring significant sacrifices. Tobacco is an expenditure that can be a source of net income as well as a means of avoiding future medical expenses. Wearing last year's clothes and enjoying less-expensive forms of entertainment are other obligations that can be considered discretionary. It is how we allocate our disposable income that determines our financial health.

CONSUMER INCOME STATEMENT		
GROSS INCOME		
Minus	Personal Taxes	
Equals	**DISPOSABLE INCOME**	
Minus	Fixed Obligations	
	•	*Housing*
	•	*Transportation*
	•	*Health care*
	•	*Other*
Minus	Variable Obligations	
	•	*Housing*
	•	*Transportation*
	•	*Food*
	•	*Health care*
	•	*Other*
Minus	Discretionary Obligations	
	•	*Apparel and services*
	•	*Entertainment*
	•	*Tobacco*
Equals	**NET INCOME**	

Table. 3-1   Sources of consumer income and expense categories on which income is spent.

In the aggregate, consumers had $61,774 in disposable income and expenditures of $50,846 in 2008. This resulted in a surplus of $11,288 or 18.3 percent of their after-tax income. For individuals trying to determine their financial health, aggregate numbers have minimal utility. If one stratifies the data by age group, one would observe that those under twenty-five years had disposable income of $27,907 and expenditures of $29,325. This resulted in a deficit of $1,418 or minus 5.1 percent of their after-tax income. Those between thirty-five and forty-four years had a surplus of $16,869 (22.3 percent of their after-tax income) and those between forty-five and fifty-four years had a surplus of $17,358 (22.1 percent of their after-tax income). Peak earning years result in the ability to save a significant portion of after-tax income.

These findings should not be surprising. Those who start to assume responsibility for themselves must incur expenses for things such as furniture, automobiles, insurance, etc., associated with their newfound independence. Those in their peak earning years have reached a point in their lives when many of their former expenses, such as those associated with raising a family, have diminished. Finally, as one retires, many have paid off their mortgages and have reduced their expenditures commensurate with the reduction in their disposable income. Those prudent consumers who allocate their surpluses to building a safety net to meet unforeseen financial needs and a retirement fund can feel proud of themselves for being financially healthy. Those who are less prudent expose themselves and their families to unncessary financial risks. Overindebteness can be hazardous to one's financial health.

DISPOSABLE INCOME VS. EXPENDITURES BY AGE
(2008)

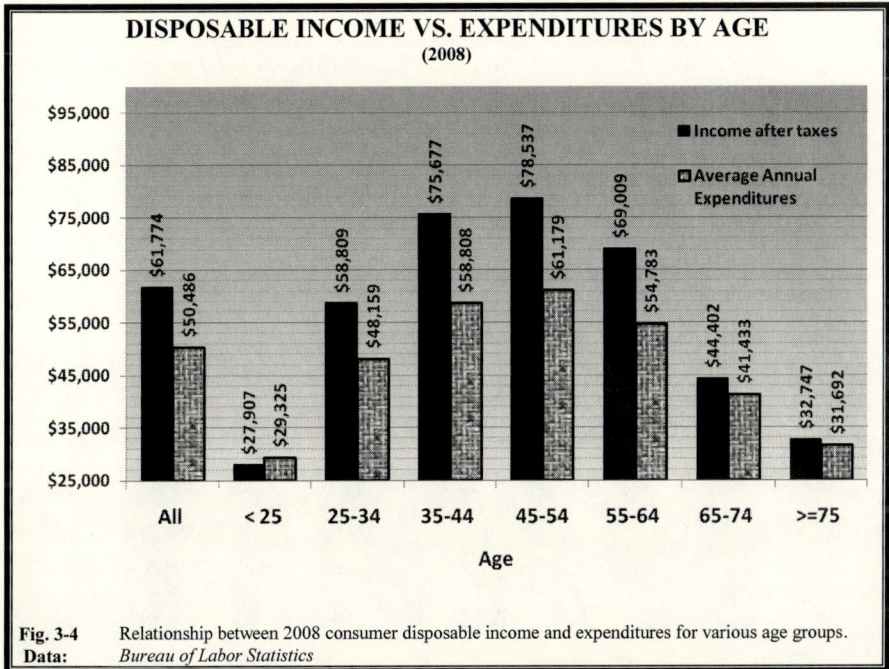

Fig. 3-4   Relationship between 2008 consumer disposable income and expenditures for various age groups.
Data: *Bureau of Labor Statistics*

Another way of examining consumer expenditures is to stratify the data by income. Unsuprisingly, those with higher incomes allocated less of their after-tax income to their annual expenditures. In 2008, consumers, in the aggregate, had after-tax income of $61.8 thousand and expenditures of $50.5 thousand, a surplus of $11.3 thousand or 18.3 percent of their after-tax income. Those with after-tax income of less than $40.0 thousand actually had expenditures that exceeded their after-tax income. For those with after-tax income between $5.0 and $10.0 thousand their expenditures exceeded their after-tax income by 132.8 percent; between $10.0 and $15.0 thousand by 61.0 percent; between $15 and $20.0 thousand by 43.1 percent; between $20 and $30 thousand by 19.8 percent; and between $30.0 and $40.0 thousand by 2.1 percent. Those earning between $40.0 and $50.0

thousand had a surplus of 9.2 percent and those earning between $50.0 and $70.0 thousand a surplus of 13.9 percent. Those fortunate enough to have earned more than $70.0 thousand averaged $123.3 thousand in after-tax income and annual expenditures of $83.7 thousand or 67.9 percent of their after-tax income. Certainly, the rich are different from the rest of us in that they, in the aggregate, are able to save considerable amounts of money. At the other extreme, those at the bottom of the economic spectrum must be subsidized in order to subsist.

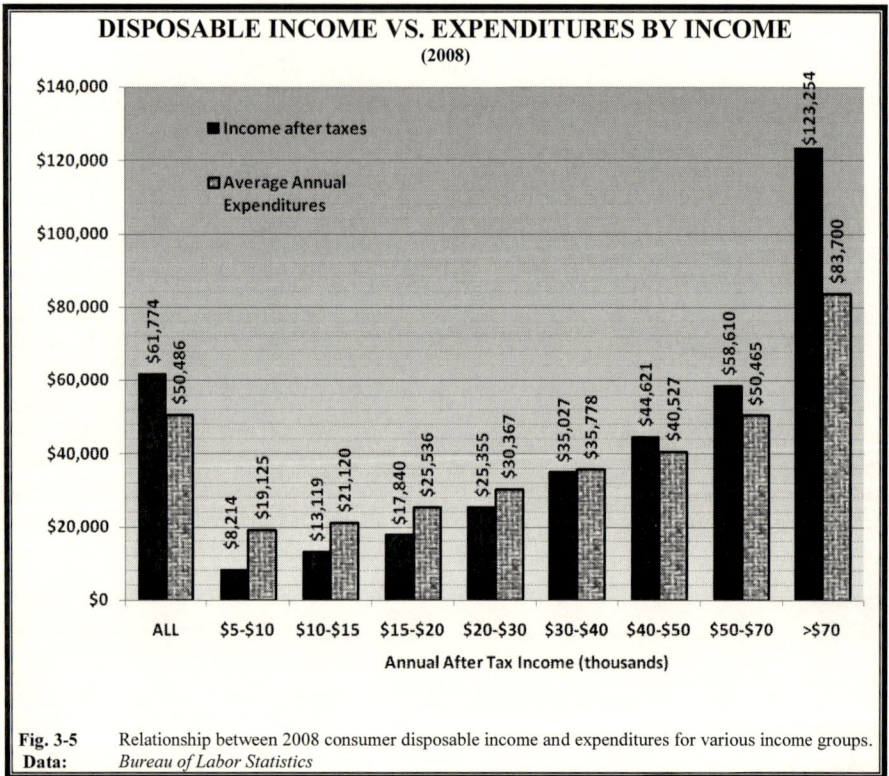

DISPOSABLE INCOME VS. EXPENDITURES BY INCOME
(2008)

Fig. 3-5 Relationship between 2008 consumer disposable income and expenditures for various income groups.
Data: *Bureau of Labor Statistics*

If one stratifies consumer units into homeowner versus renter and urban dweller versus rural dweller, one would notice that in all of these categories, after tax 2008 income exceeded expenditures. In the aggregate, 18.3 percent of consumer unit after-tax income ($11.3 thousand) remained after accounting for expenditures. Homeowners had $74.6 thousand in after-tax income and expenditures of $58.8 thousand, which represents a surplus of $11.3 thousand or 21.1 percent of their after-tax income. Renters had considerably less after-tax income and resulting surplus than homeowners. Subtracting expenditures of $34 thousand from their after-tax income of $36.4 thousand resulted in a surplus of $2.4 thousand or 6.7 percent of after-tax income. Urban consumer units had higher after-tax income and surplus funds than rural consumer units. The surplus for urban consumer units was $11.8 thousand or 18.7 percent of after-tax income; for rural homeowners $6.3 thousand or 12.5 percent of after-tax income.

DISPOSABLE INCOME VS. EXPENDITURES BY HOUSING TENURE
(2008)

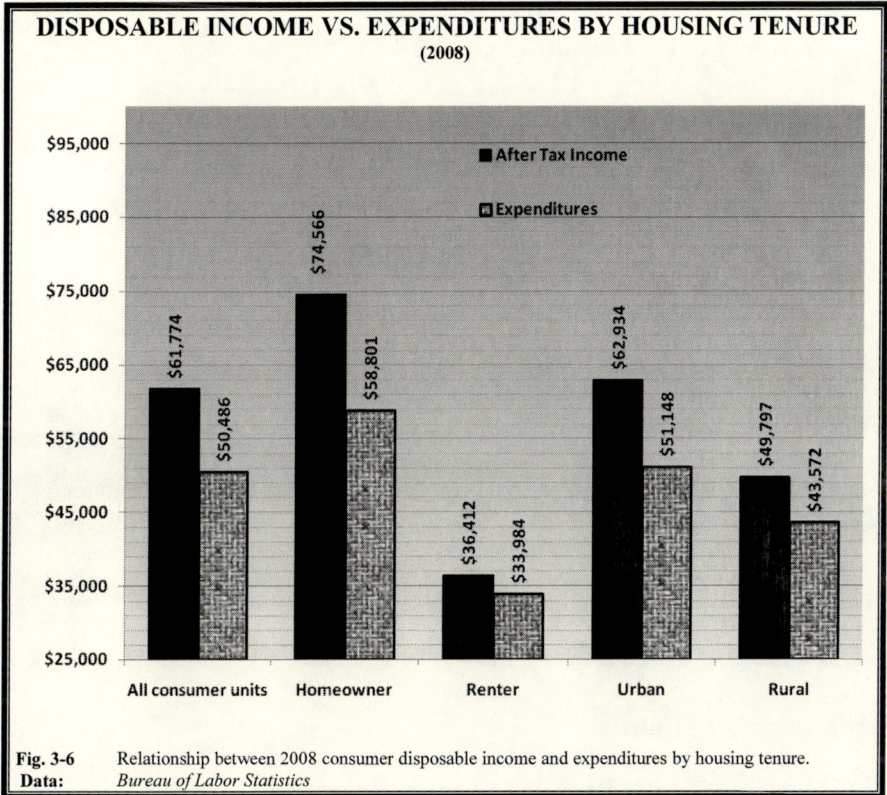

■ After Tax Income

☐ Expenditures

All consumer units: $61,774 / $50,486
Homeowner: $74,566 / $58,801
Renter: $36,412 / $33,984
Urban: $62,934 / $51,148
Rural: $49,797 / $43,572

Fig. 3-6 Relationship between 2008 consumer disposable income and expenditures by housing tenure.
Data: *Bureau of Labor Statistics*

In 2008, there were sizable differences in disposable income between regions of the United States. Households in the Northeast had disposable income of $68.2 thousand, in the West $65.4 thousand, in the Midwest $59.8 thousand, and in the South $57.5 thousand. Their respective expenditures in that same year were $54.9 thousand (80.5 percent of disposable income), $55.5 thousand (84.7 percent of disposable income), $47.8 thousand (80.0 percent of disposable income), and $46.8 thousand (81.4 percent of disposable income). Despite the differences in disposable income between regions, there were relatively minor differences in the percent of after-tax income required to support household expenditures.

DISPOSABLE INCOME VS. EXPENDITURES BY REGION
(2008)

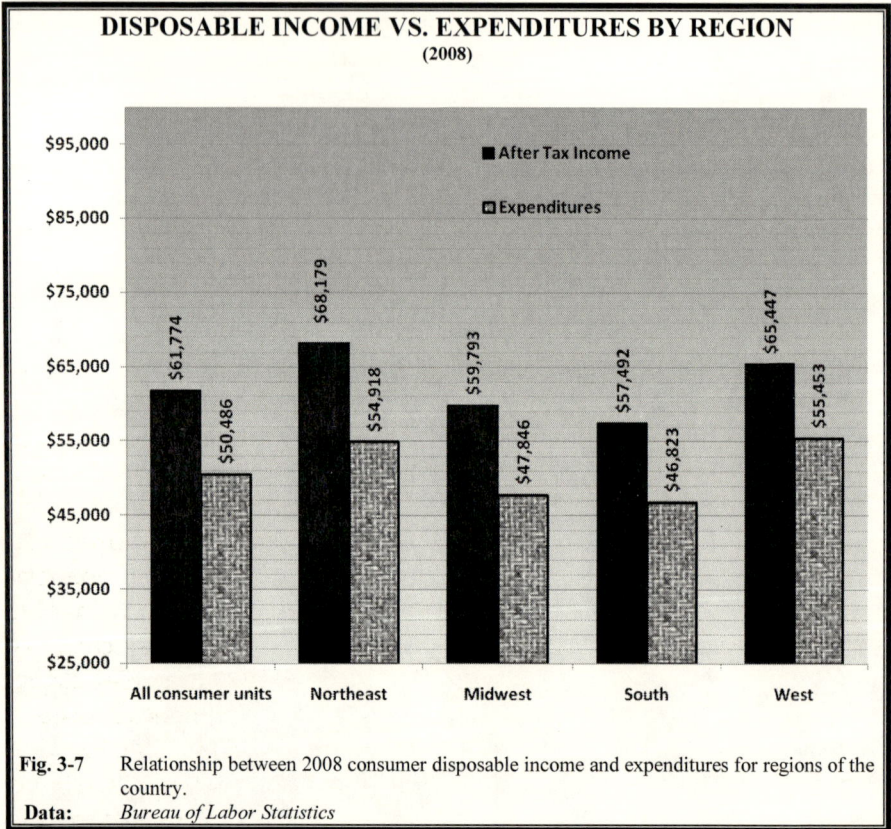

	After Tax Income	Expenditures
All consumer units	$61,774	$50,486
Northeast	$68,179	$54,918
Midwest	$59,793	$47,846
South	$57,492	$46,823
West	$65,447	$55,453

Fig. 3-7   Relationship between 2008 consumer disposable income and expenditures for regions of the country.
Data: *Bureau of Labor Statistics*

Statement of Financial Condition

Physicians determine the health of their patients based on their vital signs along with noninvasive and, when approppriate, invasive tests. Accountants measure the financial health of businesses based, in part, on their balance sheets, which are a snapshot in time of their finanicial condition. In particular, they examine the relationship between short-term obligations and the short-term assets that can be used to satisfy those short liabilities. In addition, they determine the net worth of the business and its capital structure, i.e., the relationship between debt and equity. For consumers, it is the relationship between their financial obligations and the assets they have to satisfy those obligations that determines their financial health, i.e., their net worth, which is the difference between their total assets and total obligations.

The statement of financial condition inventories assets based on their liquidity, the associated financial obligations, the time frame in which they are due, and the degree of control that the consumer unit has over them. Consumer assets can be segmented into two categories, current assets and long-term assets. Current assets are those that can be used to satisfy current obligations that are due within the next thirty days. The most liquid or readily available asset is cash, which consists of what is held in checking, savings, and money market accounts. Short-term investments, such as savings bonds and certificates of deposit, can be liquidated within a relatively short period of time. However, there may be associated losses and/or penalties from liquidating these investments prior to maturity. Long-term assets are those that can be liquidated at some time in the future to satisfy obligations that are due beyond thirty days. These long-term assets have varying degrees of liquidity or ease with which they can be converted into cash. The most liquid of these long-term assets are financial assets such as bonds, stocks, and investment funds. Other financial assets, such as life insurance along with other managed and financial assets as well as retirement funds, can be more difficult or expensive to tap as a source of unforeseen financial needs. It should be noted that liquidating retirement assets may involve penalties for early withdrawal and tax liabilities. The last category of long-term assets consists of nonfinancial assets such as real estate, vehicles, equity positions in businesses, and other nonfinancial assets.

Financial obligations consist of current obligations that are due within the next thirty days and long-term obligations that can extend for months or years. Current obligations include the costs of the following:

- Housing such as shelter, utilities, furnishings and equipment, operations, and supplies
- Transportation such as vehicle purchases, gasoline and motor oil, vehicle insurance, vehicle maintenance and repairs, public transportation, vehicle finance charges, and other vehicle expenses
- Food consumed at home and away from home
- Entertainment such as audiovisual equipment and services, fees and admissions, pets, toys, hobbies and playground equipment, and others

- Apparel and services such as women's and girls' apparel, men's and boys' apparel, footwear, apparel for children under two, and others
- Health care such as health insurance, medical services, drugs, and medical supplies
- Other items such as cash contributions, pensions, education, alcoholic beverages, personal care products and services, tobacco, life and other personal insurance, reading, and miscellaneous

Long-term financial obligations such as mortgages, home equity loans or lines of credit, and other residential real estate debt can extend for as long as thirty years. Installment loans for vehicles, education, etc., can extend over several months and years. Other long-term financial obligations include unpaid credit card balances as well as other lines of credit and debt. In the perfect world, current obligations would be satisfied by available cash in the form of checking, savings, and money market accounts. In the less-than-perfect world, it might be necessary to liquidate a portion of short-term investments such as savings bonds and certificates of deposit to meet those obligations. Expressed as a numerical measure, a perfect current position would be one in which the ratio of cash to total current obligations is greater than or equal to one. A healthy financial condition would be one in which the ratio of total current assets to total current obligations was greater than or equal to one. In each case, the greater the ratio, the better the current position. Net worth is what remains after all financial obligations have been deducted from total assets. The higher the net worth, the healthier the financial position is.

STATEMENT OF FINANCIAL CONDITION	
ASSETS	**FINANCIAL OBLIGATIONS**
CURRENT ASSETS	**CURRENT OBLIGATIONS**
Cash	Housing
Short-Term Investments	Transportation
	Food
	Entertainment
	Apparel and Services
	Health Care
	Other
LONG-TERM ASSETS	**LONG-TERM OBLIGATIONS**
Financial Assets	Home-Secured Debt
Retirements Accounts	Installment Loans
Nonfinancial Assets	Credit Card Balances
	Other Lines of Credit
	Other Debt
	NET WORTH

Table 3-2   Relationship between various categories of consumer unit assets and financial obligations.

Quaestrological Measures

Net Worth

Perhaps the most basic of quaestrological measures is net worth, the difference between assets and liabilities. Too often, people judge their financial situation based on what they have and neglect the debt that had been used to obtain those assets. In 2008, the financial condition of the United States consumer unit exhibited a deterioration in his/her net worth. The net change in liabilities exceeded the net change in assets for all those included in the survey conducted by the Bureau of Labor Statistics. Net liabilities increased by $11,421 as net assets increased by $7,349. This represented a decrease in net worth of $4,072. It should be noted that the net worth of all consumer units headed by someone under sixty-four years of age decreased as their net liabilities increased faster than their net assets. The deterioration ranged from $43 for those consumer units whose head was under twenty-five years to as high as $8,594 for those whose head was between forty-five and fifty-four years. It is ironic that this latter age group experienced a detioration in net worth in what was its peak earning years. Those past the retirement age of sixty-five years actually saw their net worth increase. This phenomenon probably has more due to with their minimizing increases in net liabilities rather than increasing their net assets.

CHANGES IN NET WORTH BY AGE
(2008)

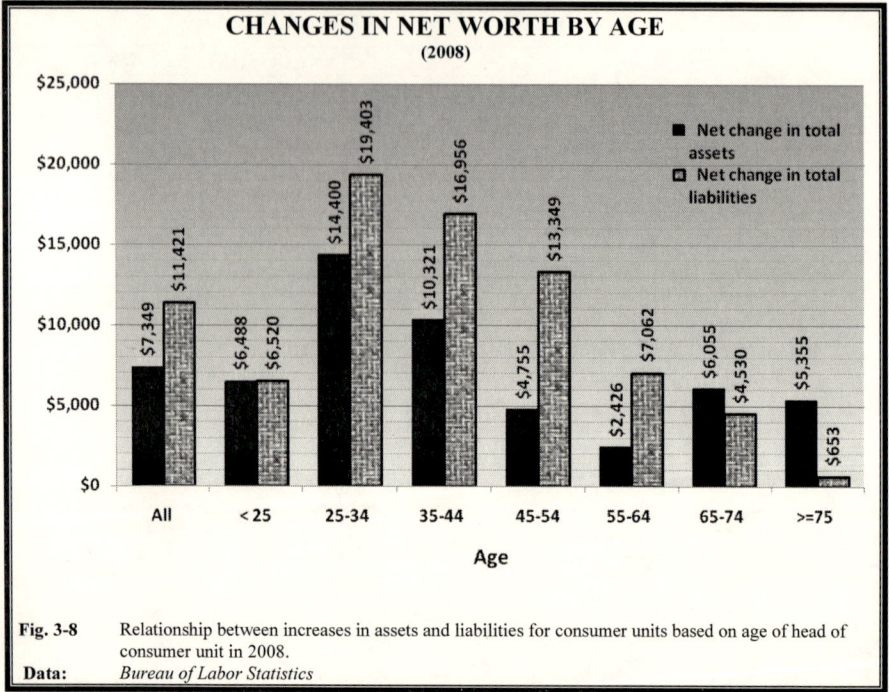

Fig. 3-8 Relationship between increases in assets and liabilities for consumer units based on age of head of consumer unit in 2008.

Data: *Bureau of Labor Statistics*

Stratifying consumer units by income level reveals that only those earning less than $10,000 per year in 2008 and those earning between $40,000 and $50,000 experienced increases in their net worth. Their net worth increased by $419 and $594 respectively that year. The deterioration in the net worth of the other income levels ranged from $387 for those earning bteween $10,000 and $5,000 to $9,235 for those earning over $70,000.

CHANGES IN NET WORTH BY INCOME
(2008)

	Net change in total assets	Net change in total liabilities
ALL	$7,349	$11,421
$5-$10	$2,467	$2,048
$10-$15	$1,888	$2,275
$15-$20	$425	$2,525
$20-$30	$3,910	$5,026
$30-$40	$3,669	$5,137
$40-$50	$3,738	$3,144
$50-$70	$6,477	$9,769
>$70	$15,169	$24,404

Annual After Tax Income (thousands)

Fig. 3-9 Relationship between increases in assets and liabilities for various income groups in 2008.
Data: *Bureau of Labor Statistics*

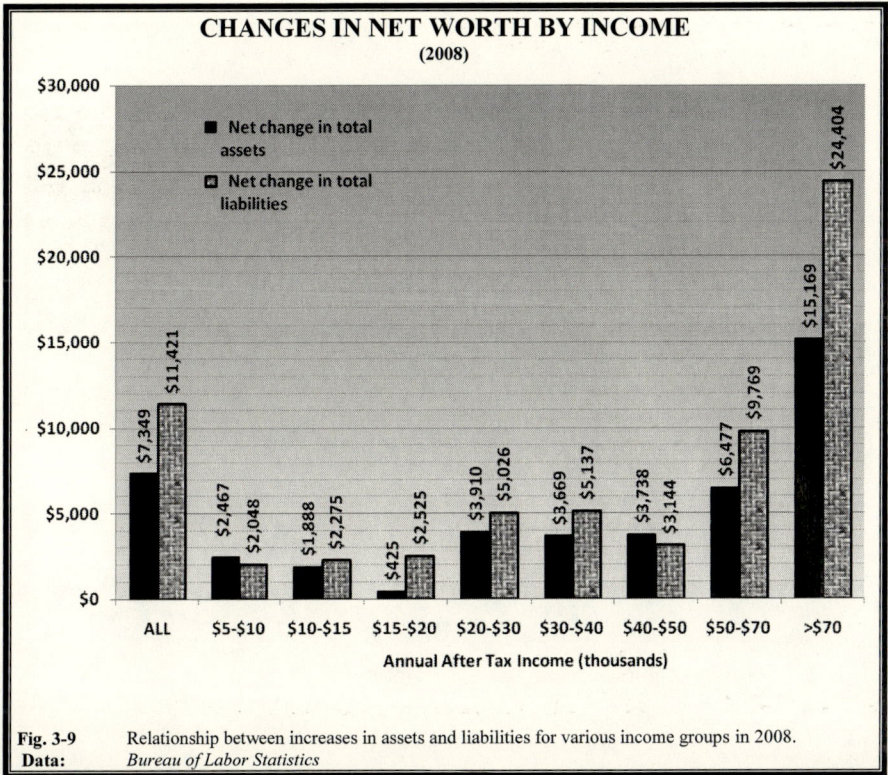

If one were to look at the effect that housing tenure has on consumer unit net worth, one would learn that all consumer units, irrespective of housing tenure, experienced a decrease in their net worth in 2008. While the net worth of homeowners decreased by $5,850 in 2008, that of renters decreased by $547. For urban consumer units, net worth decreased $4,382. For rural households, it decreased by $876.

CHANGES IN NET WORTH BY HOUSING TENURE
(2008)

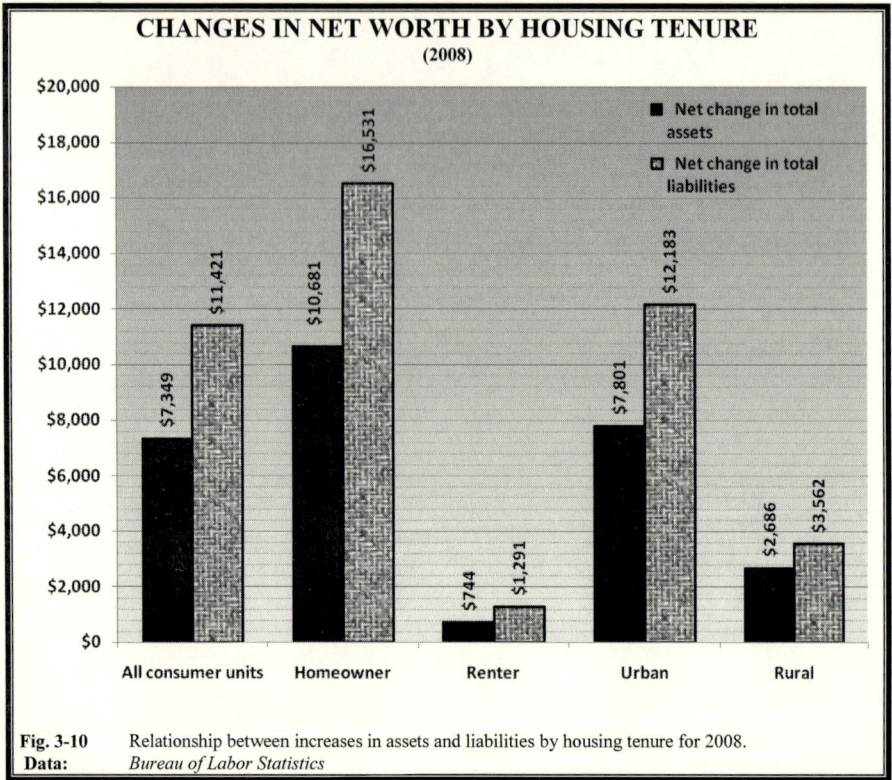

Fig. 3-10   Relationship between increases in assets and liabilities by housing tenure for 2008.
Data: *Bureau of Labor Statistics*

There was a significant disparity decrease in consumer unit net worth based on the region of the country in which the consumer unit resided. In the South, net worth decreased by $1,063, in the Midwest by $3,504, in the Northeast by $4,756, and in the West by $8,970.

CHANGES IN NET WORTH BY REGION
(2008)

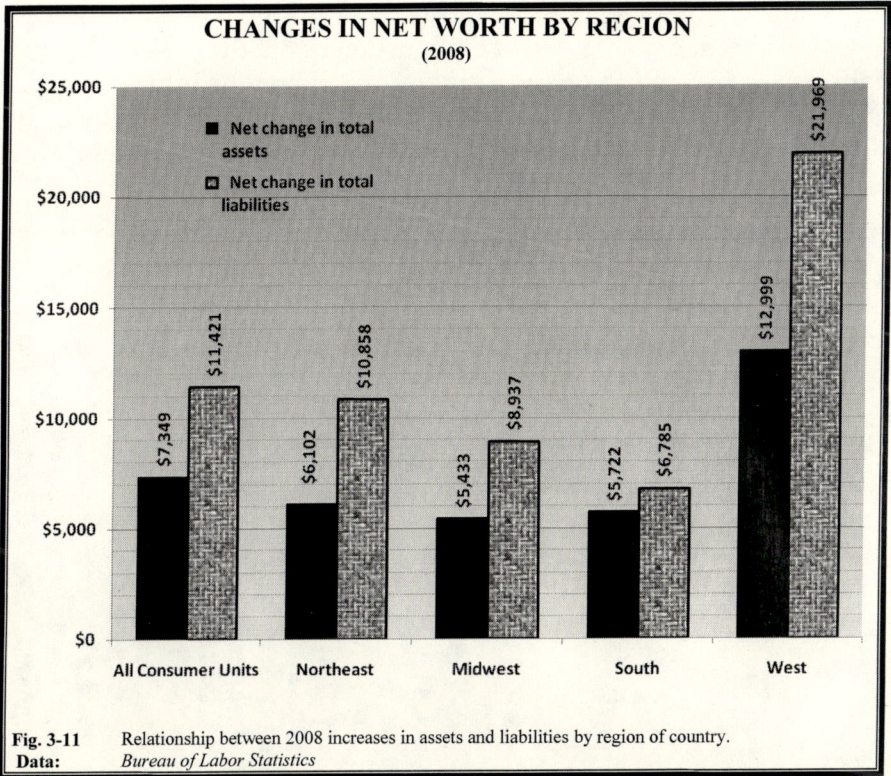

Fig. 3-11 Relationship between 2008 increases in assets and liabilities by region of country.
Data: *Bureau of Labor Statistics*

Net Income

Very simply stated, net income is the amount of money that is available after all the income-related taxes and financial obligations have been satisfied over a given period of time. In certain periods of time, there may be sufficient income to cover our obligations; in other periods, there may not be. Income that exceeds obligations is called a surplus; income that is exceeded by obligations is called a deficit. The significance of a surplus or deficit is relative to the amount of income. A $1,000 surplus is significant against a gross income of $10,000 but is insignificant as compared to a gross income of $100,000. For this reason, net income needs to always be evaluated as a percentage of gross income.

Despite all the concerns about consumer spending habits, there has been a significant improvement in the amount of money left after accounting for expenses. In 1984, consumer units had a deficit of $738; by 1990, it became a surplus of $556; by 2000, the surplus grew to $3,487; and by 2008, it was $11,288. It should be noted that these numbers reflect the changes in net income for all consumer units irrespective of their gross income, age of the head of the consumer unit; the consumer unit's housing tenure, and the region of the country in which the consumer unit resided. The proverbial caveat that actual experiences may differ surely applies to this data as a significant number of consumer units have actually experienced deficits.

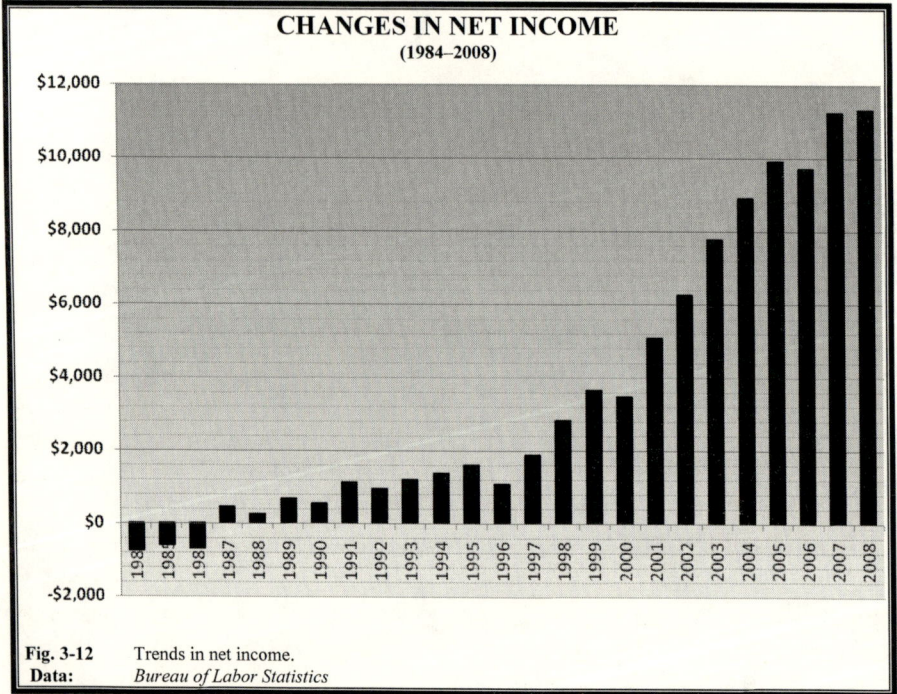

CHANGES IN NET INCOME
(1984–2008)

Fig. 3-12 Trends in net income.
Data: *Bureau of Labor Statistics*

Income Obligations

The relationship between consumer unit income and obligations is measured by the following:

- Fixed obligations coverage, which is the ratio of monthly gross income to the fixed obligations due in the current month
- Variable obligations coverage, which is the ratio of monthly gross income to the variable obligations due in the current month
- Discretionary obligations coverage, which is the ratio of monthly gross income to the discretionary obligations due in the current month

- Income surplus (deficit), which is the ratio of monthly gross income to the amount of income that that remains after meeting that month's fixed, variable, and discretionary financial obligations

The relationships between consumer unit income and its financial obligations improved in all categories from 1989 to 2007. Fixed income coverage improved from 2.8:1 to 2.9:1, variable obligations coverage from 2.6:1 to 3.0:1, discretionary obligations coverage from 6.5:1 to 8.4:1. Surplus income increased from 0.1:1 to 0.2:1.

CHANGES IN INCOME OBLIGATIONS (1989–2007)							
	1989	1992	1995	1998	2001	2004	2007
FIXED OBLIGATIONS COVERAGE	2.8	2.8	2.8	2.8	2.8	2.9	2.9
VARIABLE OBLIGATIONS COVERAGE	2.6	2.7	2.7	2.8	2.9	3.0	3.0
DISCRETIONARY OBLIGATIONS COVERAGE	6.5	6.5	6.8	7.4	7.9	8.5	8.4
INCOME SURPLUS (DEFICIT)	0.1	0.1	0.1	0.1	0.2	0.2	0.2

Table 3-3 Changes in ratios of consumer unit gross income to its financial obligations.
Data: *2007 Federal Reserve Survey Consumer Finances*
Bureau of Labor Statistics

Current Assets

The purpose of current assets is to have available funds to be used to meet financial obligations that cannot be satisfied with current income. Current assets are:

- Cash, which consists of funds held in checking, savings, and money market checking accounts.
- Short-term investments are funds held in certificates of deposit and savings bonds. Included within these short-term investments are the safety net funds, which are reserves established to be used in case of extraordinary expenses or loss of income.

From 1989 to 2007, the percent of consumer units that had cash assets increased from 85.5 percent to 92.1 percent. The dollar value of those cash assets increased from $23.2 thousand to $26.4 thousand. During that same time period, the percent of consumer units that had certificates of deposit and savings bonds declined. In 1989, 19.9 percent of consumer units had certificates of deposit and 23.9 percent had savings bonds. By 2007, 16.1 percent had certificates of deposit and 14.9 percent savings bonds. Despite the decline in the percent of consumer units holding these assets, the value of these holdings increased. Investments in certificates of deposit increased from $53.3 to $55.6 thousand; in savings bonds $6.5 to $6.6 thousand.

CHANGES IN CURRENT ASSETS (1989–2007)								
		1989	1992	1995	1998	2001	2004	2007
CASH	%	85.5	86.9	87.4	90.6	91.4	91.3	92.1
	$	23.2	20.0	19.6	21.4	27.7	29.8	26.4
SHORT-TERM INVESTMENTS								
• Certificates of	%	19.9	16.7	14.3	15.3	15.7	12.7	16.1
Deposit	$	53.3	47.8	48.5	47.9	43.8	60.2	55.6
• Savings Bonds	%	23.9	22.3	22.8	19.3	16.7	17.6	14.9
	$	6.5	5.1	7.1	6.0	9.2	6.3	6.6

Table 3-4 Changes in percent of consumer units having current assets and the mean value of those assets in thousands of dollars.
Data: *2007 Federal Reserve Survey Consumer Finances*

Long-Term Assets

Long-term assets are comprised of financial, retirement, and nonfinancial assets. They are investments that are designated to meet future strategic needs such as purchasing a home, sending children to college, or saving for retirement. The shorter the time frame in which the funds will be needed, the more certainty of principal outweighs potential returns.

Financial assets consist of stocks, bonds, pooled investment funds, cash-value life insurance, along with other managed and financial assets. From 1989 to 2007, the percent of consumer units that had financial assets increased from 88.9 to 93.9. The mean value of these assets increased from $117.1 to $237.4 thousand. An examination of the various classes of financial assets held by consumer units during that same time period reveals that despite decreases in the percent of consumer units that owned bonds, cash-value life insurance, and other financial assets, there were increases in the mean value of all their financial assets.

CHANGES IN FINANCIAL ASSETS
(1989–2007)

		1989	1992	1995	1998	2001	2004	2007
FINANCIAL ASSETS	%	88.9	90.3	91.2	93.1	93.4	93.8	93.9
	$000	117.1	110.6	135.3	183.8	238.7	221.7	237.4
Directly Held Stocks	%	16.8	17.0	15.2	19.2	21.3	20.7	17.9
	$000	92.8	96.6	126.2	202.2	224.9	176.1	221.1
Directly Held Bonds	%	5.7	4.3	3.1	3.0	3.0	1.8	1.6
	$000	186.2	197.1	250.0	247.1	340.7	600.8	574.3
Pooled Investment Funds	%	7.2	10.4	12.3	16.5	17.7	15.0	11.4
	$000	76.6	73.0	126.9	128.6	152.9	202.0	309.7
Cash-Value Life Insurance	%	35.5	34.9	32.0	29.6	28.0	24.2	23.0
	$000	17.5	17.0	27.7	36.7	42.2	25.3	31.3
Other Managed Assets	%	3.6	4.0	3.9	5.9	6.6	7.3	5.8
	$000	188.5	135.2	184.1	246.5	353.1	227.4	248.8
Other Financial Assets	%	13.8	10.8	11.1	9.4	9.4	10.0	9.3
	$000	36.1	34.6	37.0	30.5	46.0	43.4	50.3

Table 3-5   Changes in percent of consumer units having financial assets and the mean value in thousands of dollars.
Data: *2007 Federal Reserve Survey Consumer Finances*

Retirement accounts are funds that are invested so that they can provide income to support the consumer unit's living expenses during retirement. These funds should not be used to support current consumer unit's financial obligations. From 1989 to 2007, the percentage of consumer units that had retirement accounts increased by 42.8 percent (37.1 to 53.0 percent). The retirement assets of consumer units that had retirement accounts increased by 144.8 percent ($60.3 to $147.6 thousand).

CHANGES IN RETIREMENT ASSETS
(1989–2007)

		1989	1992	1995	1998	2001	2004	2007
RETIREMENT ASSETS	%	37.1	40.1	45.3	48.9	52.8	49.9	53.0
	$000	60.3	64.3	77.0	97.1	122.5	135.2	147.6

Table 3-6   Changes in percent of consumer units having retirement accounts and the mean value of those accounts in thousands of dollars.
Data: *2007 Federal Reserve Survey Consumer Finances*

Nonfinancial assets consist of primary residence, other residential real estate, vehicles, and net equity in nonresidential real estate, business equity, and other nonfinancial assets. Due to their nature, their values are somewhat subjective and may take weeks, months, or longer to sell. The percentage of consumer units that had nonfinancial assets is not appreciably different from those that had financial assets (92.0 vs. 93.9 percent in 2007). However, the value of their nonfinancial assets was approximately twice that of their financial assets ($469.5 vs. $237.4 thousand in 2007). From 1989 to 2007, the value of the nonfinancial assets owned by consumer units increased substantially. Vehicles owned increased the least, 39.2 percent, while other residential real estate the most, 128.0 percent. Only two nonfinancial assets exhibited a decrease in consumer units' ownership, equity in nonresidential real estate and other nonfinancial assets.

CHANGES IN NONFINANCIAL ASSETS
(1989–2007)

		1989	1992	1995	1998	2001	2004	2007
NONFINANCIAL	%	89.3	90.8	90.9	89.9	90.7	92.5	92.0
ASSETS	$000	265.6	237.7	233.6	276.7	336.7	402.3	469.5
Primary Residence	%	63.9	63.9	64.7	66.2	67.7	69.1	68.6
	$000	170.5	158.6	155.7	176.6	211.5	271.1	302.4
Owned Vehicles	%	83.8	86.1	84.1	82.8	84.8	86.3	87.0
	$000	15.8	14.3	18.0	19.4	21.4	22.1	22.0
Other Residential Real Estate	%	13.1	12.7	11.8	12.8	11.3	12.5	13.7
	$000	147.2	144.2	143.5	164.9	217.9	293.6	335.6
Equity in Nonresidential Real Estate	%	11.1	9.5	9.2	8.5	8.2	8.3	8.1
	$000	236.0	249.3	181.9	225.5	304.3	327.4	309.4
Business Equity	%	13.3	14.3	12.8	12.7	13.5	13.3	13.6
	$000	476.4	395.3	452.3	560.0	660.3	723.0	946.3
Other Nonfinancial Assets	%	12.4	8.3	9.0	8.5	7.5	7.8	7.2
	$000	47.7	42.5	54.3	51.4	66.1	73.1	80.7

Table 3-7   Changes in percent of consumer units having nonfinancial assets and the mean value in thousands of dollars.
Data: *2007 Federal Reserve Survey Consumer Finances*

Liquidity Ratios

There are two ratios that measure consumer ability to satisfy current obligations. They are:

- The current ratio as applied to the consumer indicates the extent to which there are sufficient current assets to satisfy current obligations. At a minimum, it should be at least one, which means that current financial obligations can be satisfied by current assets.

- The acid-test ratio measures the ability to satisfy current obligations with current income.

Consumers should seek to cover their monthly obligations with their monthly income (acid test). If monthly income is insufficient to cover that month's financial obligations, cash assets and their short-term investments should be available to satisfy unusual financial obligations, such as repair bills, that occur from time to time. Another way of looking at these ratios is to consider short-term investments and cash assets that are left over after satisfying current financial obligations as a safety net to be used to cover financial emergencies.

From 1989 to 2007, there was dichotomy in the trends of consumer unit liquidity ratios. The current ratio declined from 13.8:1 to 8.1:1 while the acid test increased from 1.1:1 to 1.3:1.

CHANGES IN LIQUIDITY RATIOS
(1989–2007)

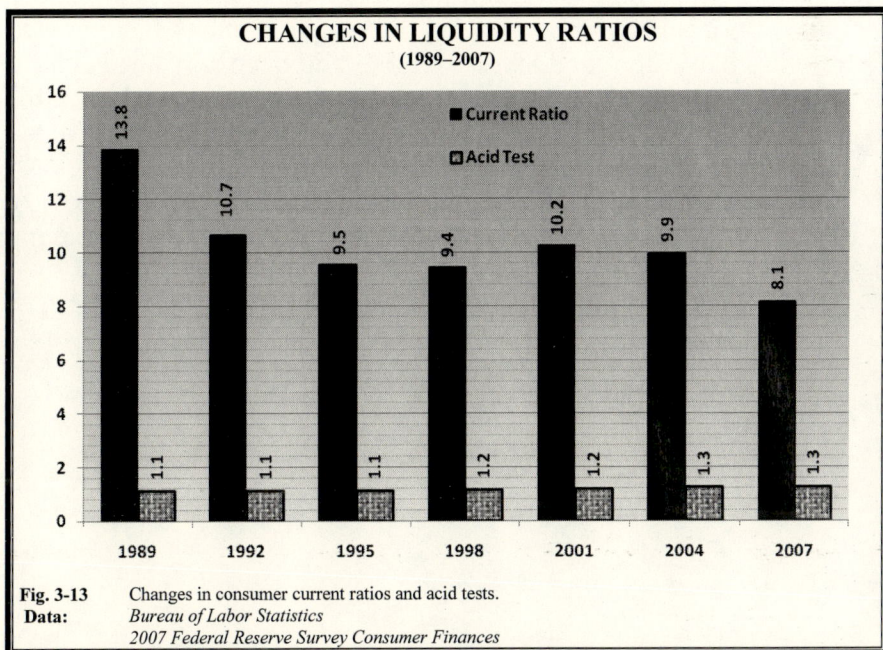

Fig. 3-13	Changes in consumer current ratios and acid tests.
Data:	*Bureau of Labor Statistics*
	2007 Federal Reserve Survey Consumer Finances

Indebtedness Ratios

There are three measurements used by the Federal Reserve Board to measure consumer indebtedness that can be used to determine the state of our quaestrology. They are the following:

- Debt service ratio (DSR), which is an estimate of all outstanding mortgage and consumer debt payments to disposable income
- Financial obligation ratio (FOR), which adds automobile lease payments, rental payments on tenant-occupied property, homeowners' insurance, and property tax payments to the DSR
- Consumer debt ratio (CDR), which is an estimate of outstanding credit card and other consumer debt as compared to disposable income

The higher any of these ratios are, the greater the risk to our being able to safely meet our financial obligations with our disposable income. Conversely, the lower the ratio, the more comfortably we can pay our bills. Unfortunately, many of us, irrespective of our stage in life, have overextended ourselves by committing ourselves to financial obligations that we cannot satisfy. To compound the situation, many have treated their homes like automated teller machines and have borrowed against their home equity with the expectation that their homes will continue to increase in value. Unfortunately, the past few years have invalidated the assumption of continually appreciating home prices.

Since 1980, the debt service ratio (DSR) increased from a low of 10.61percent in 1980 to a high of 13.86 percent in 2007. Despite having decreased from 2007 to 2009, the DSR had still increased by 30.63 percent since 1980. Moreover, at the end of 2009, the DSR was still 15.50 percent higher than the median value from 1980 to 2009.

Debt Service Ratio Trend
(1980–2009)

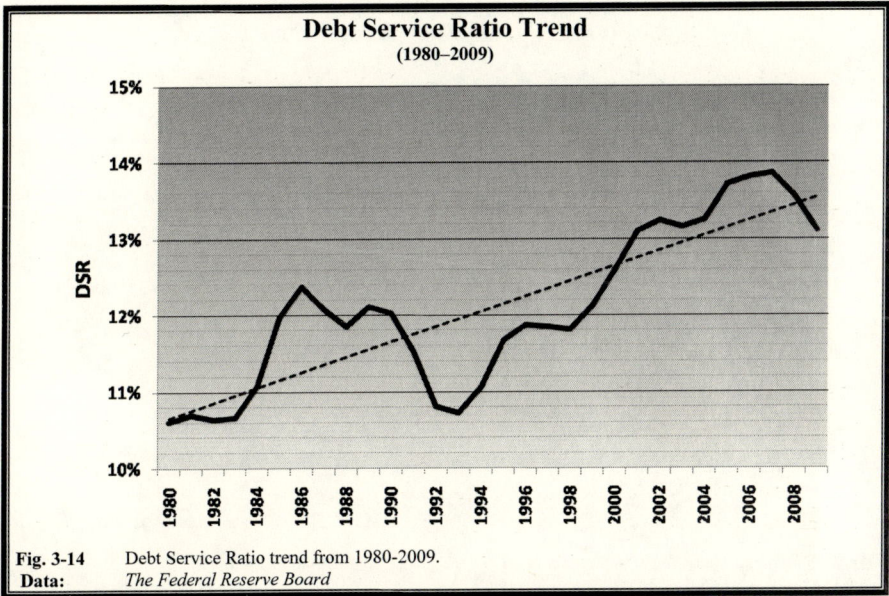

Fig. 3-14   Debt Service Ratio trend from 1980-2009.
Data: *The Federal Reserve Board*

The financial obligations ratio (FOR) is determined by adding automobile lease payments, rental payments on tenant-occupied property, homeowners' insurance, and property tax payments to the debt service ratio. Homeowner and renter FORs are calculated by applying homeowner and renter shares of payments and income derived from the Survey of Consumer Finances and Current Population Survey to the numerator and denominator of the FOR. The homeowner mortgage FOR includes payments on mortgage debt, homeowners' insurance, and property taxes, while the homeowner consumer FOR includes payments on consumer debt and automobile leases.

From their starting values in 1980 to 2007, the financial obligation ratio (FOR) for renters increased 21.5 percent while the ratio for homeowners increased by 30.5 percent. From 2007 to 2009, the FOR for renters decreased by 3.8 percent; for homeowners by 4.8 percent. At the end of 2009, the renter FOR stood at 4.1 percent of the 1980–2009 median value; the homeowner at 9.8 percent.

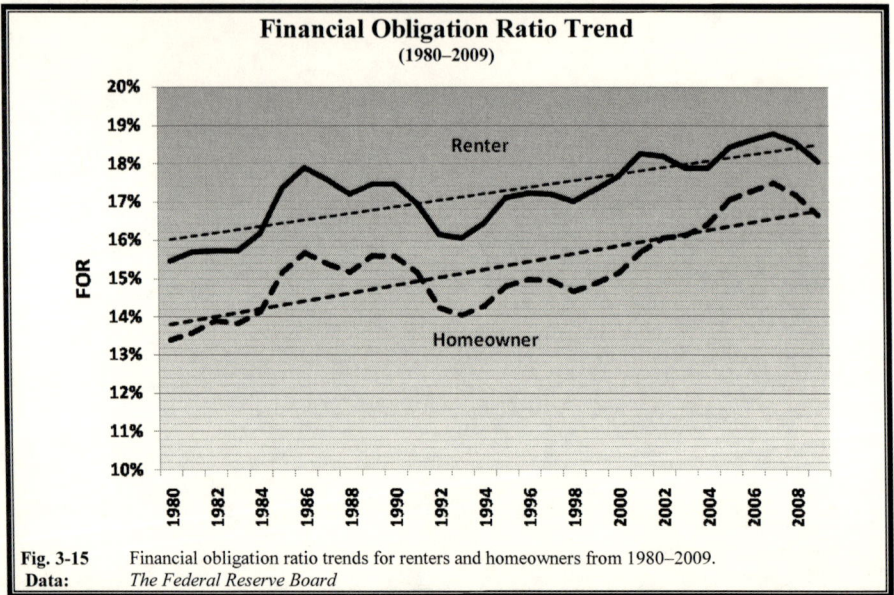

Financial Obligation Ratio Trend
(1980–2009)

Fig. 3-15   Financial obligation ratio trends for renters and homeowners from 1980–2009.
Data: *The Federal Reserve Board*

The consumer debt ratio (CDR) oscillated between 4.56 percent and 6.64 percent from 1980–2009. It reached its nadir in 1992 at 4.56 percent and its zenith in 2002 at 6.64 percent, an increase of 45.61 percent. As was the case with DSR and FOR, the CDR has declined in recent years. Yet at the end of 2009, it was 1.57 percent above its median value of 5.73 percent.

Consumer indebtedness can also be expressed by comparing the total outstanding balances of consumer debt to annual disposable income. At the end of 2009, the consumer debt of the average American consumer unit was 122.0 percent of annual disposable income. Many economists believe that any ratio that exceeds 100.0 percent is an unsustainable level of debt.

Consumer Debt Ratio Trend
(1980–2009)

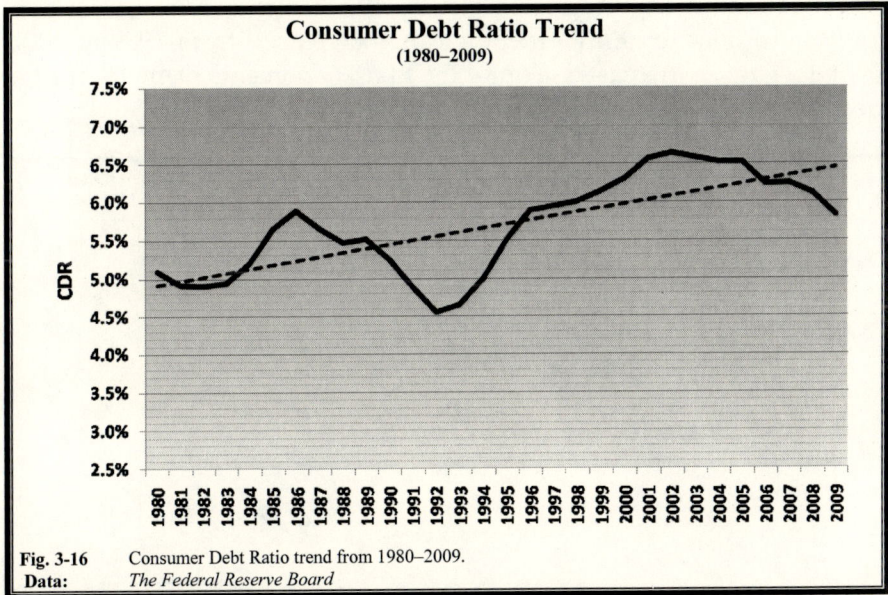

Fig. 3-16   Consumer Debt Ratio trend from 1980–2009.
Data: *The Federal Reserve Board*

Leverage

While we may have a positive net worth, this is not necessarily in itself an indication of financial health. If we have debts such as mortgages, car loans, student loans, etc., that are financial obligations that we must repay over several months and/or years, we must evaluate their impact. Have we leveraged ourselves, high long-term obligations relative to our unencumbered assets? Do we have sufficient equity to satisfy these debts? The way we can answer these questions is to compare our long-term financial obligations, debts, to the current value of these assets, equity. A debt to equity ratio of more than one means that we owe more than the value of our assets. This is an indication of being highly leveraged.

Leverage, in itself, is not necessarily bad. If the value of the underlying asset appreciates, then the return on our investment of equity is improved. A $1.0 million asset that is financed by $200 thousand in equity and $800 thousand in debt and appreciates by $200 thousand would represent a 20 percent return on the $1.0 million investment and a 100 percent return on equity. However, should that asset's value decline by 20 percent that would represent a 20 percent loss on the investment and a 100 percent loss of equity.

Another way to measure leverage is to compare debt to annual income. The lower the number, the less leveraged a consumer unit is.

As the following graph illustrates, both the consumer unit debt to equity and debt to annual income ratios increased from 1989 to 2007. Debt to equity increased from 12.9 to 15.6 percent. Debt to annual income increased from 123.2 to 137.3 percent.

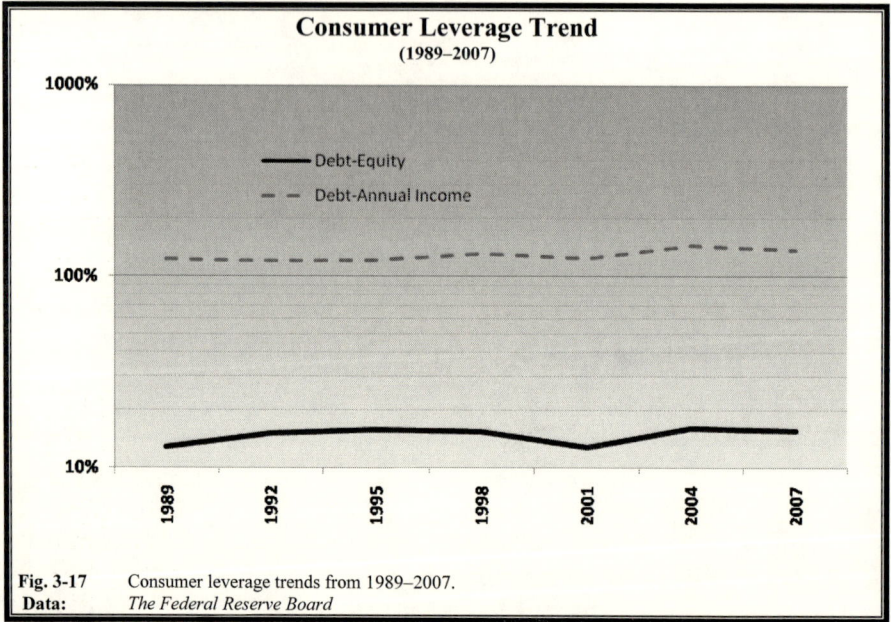

Consumer Leverage Trend
(1989–2007)

| Fig. 3-17 | Consumer leverage trends from 1989–2007. |
| Data: | *The Federal Reserve Board* |

Retirement Coverage

Since the future of Social Security and private pension funds is uncertain, it is incumbent on the individual to take responsibility for his/her individual retirement needs. Relying on Social Security, employer pensions, home equity, or a bequest from a rich relative is a risk that the prudent individual should not take. It is generally accepted by most financial planners that in order to not outlive one's retirement funds, one should not withdraw more than 4 percent of his/her funds per year. This means that, at retirement, one should have twenty-five times his/her planned retirement needs during the first year of retirement. For planning purposes, one should assume that he/she will need first-year retirement funds equal to at least his/her last year's preretirement level. While one may save on certain expenses, such as commuting costs, during retirement, other costs, such as travel and health care, may increase. Retirement funds should be measured as a percent of the ultimate amount needed at retirement. In addition, Social Security and pension income should not be considered in determining retirement funds. They should be considered as income that reduces the need to withdraw retirement funds.

The allocation of retirement assets is dependent on the time frame in which the funds will be needed. The longer the time frame, the more the risk that can be taken in seeking potentially higher returns. Conversely, the shorter the time frame, the certainty of principal outweighs any potential returns. However, under no circumstances should one invest all his/her funds in one class of investments. One should allocate assets across a spectrum of classes in order to manage risk.

While consumer units increased their retirement assets by 72.2 percent with respect to their annual income from 1989 to 2007, they were still woefully unprepared for the retirement living. In 2007, their retirement assets represented 1.2 times of their annual gross income.

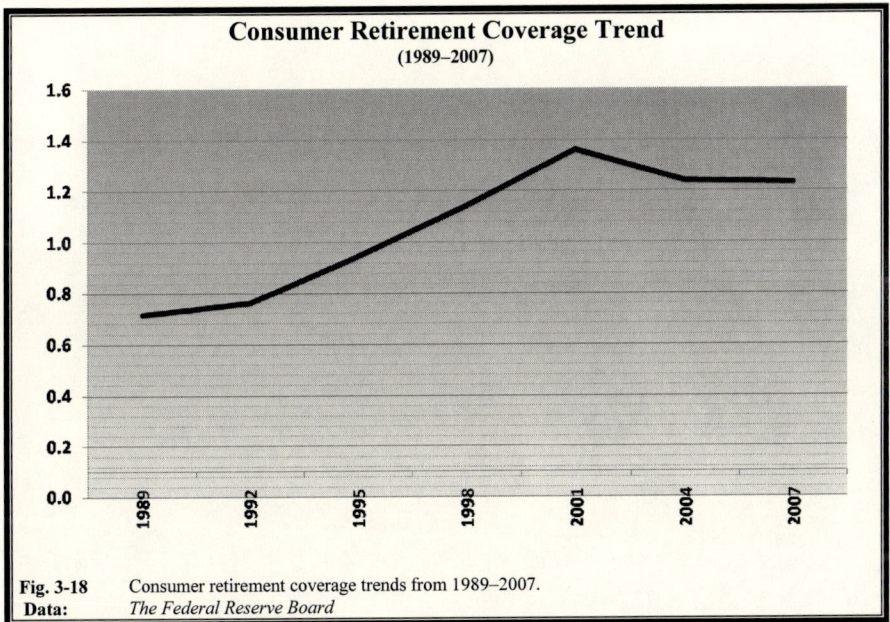

Consumer Retirement Coverage Trend
(1989–2007)

Fig. 3-18 Consumer retirement coverage trends from 1989–2007.
Data: *The Federal Reserve Board*

The preceding ratios may not apply to many of us. However, they serve as a baseline against which we can evaluate the relationship between our financial obligations, our disposable income, and our assets.

QUAESTROLOGICAL PROFILES

Obviously, there are very few consumer units, if any, that have income and expenditures as those previously discussed. Depending on one's age, income, housing tenure, and where one lives, his/her individual financial profile can vary significantly. Despite these differences, it is essential to have a baseline against which one can compare his/her quaestrology or financial health. It is the intent of this chapter to present personal financial information from a persepective that can allow one to better manage his/her finances. For purposes of providing the reader with such a baseline, 2007 data on consumer expenditures and changes in U.S. family finances prepared by the Bureau of Labor Statistics and the Federal Reserve have been used in preparing consumer income statement and summary of financial condition from which the quaestrolgical profiles are presented in this chapter. This data has been segmented based on the age of the head of consumer unit. A sufficient level of supporting detail has been provided to allow the reader to evaluate and adjust his/her own baseline quaestrological profile. In developing a quaestrological profile for one's own consumer unit, it may be necessary to adjust the ranges to reflect the income of the household, housing tenure, and the region within the country that the consumer unit lives. In addition, this chapter presents areas of opportunity for improving one's quaestrological profile.

Consumer Unit Profile

There can be significant differences between consumer units (households) depending on many factors. Perhaps the most relevant factor is the age of the head of the consumer unit. Younger consumer units tend to have more members than older ones. Consumer units headed by someone less than thirty-five years had 2.8 members of which 1.1 were under eighteen years, By contrast, consumer units headed by someone over seventy-four years had 1.5 members of which less than 0.05 were less than eighteen years. The younger consumer unit had 1.5 earners as compared to 0.2 in the older one. In addition, the number of earners per consumer unit increased from 1.5 in consumer units headed by someone less than thirty-five years to 1.7 in units headed by someone between forty-five and fifty-four years and then decreased to 0.2 in the oldest consumer units. The percentage of consumer units that were homeowners increased from 47.0 percent for those headed by someone less than thirty-five years to 81.0 percent for those between sixty-five and seventy-four years. As one might expect, the percentage of consumer units without a mortgage increased with the age of the head of the consumer unit. Consumer units headed by a younger person have different income before taxes than ones headed by an older person. Gross income increased from $57.3 thousand in consumer units headed by someone under thirty-five years to a maximum of $80.6 thousand in consumer units whose head was between forty-five and fifty-four years. In consumer units headed by someone older than seventy-four years, the income before taxes decreased to $32.5 thousand.

Consumer Income Statement

The consumer income statement depicts the sources of one's income and how that income is spent. If there is any income remaining after personal taxes and one's financial obligations have been met, one is said to have net income, which is a good thing. If, on the other hand, one's financial obligations exceed one's income, that is a bad thing. In such circumstances, one must dip into savings or incur debt to satsify one's obligations. In extreme cases, bankruptcy may be the only option. Clearly, if one has any expectations of accumulating wealth, one must have something to invest, i.e., positive net income. The more of one's income that can be saved, the better one's quaestrological profile.

Businesses classify their costs into two categories, fixed and variable. Fixed costs are those that will be incurred regardless of the level of activity and variable costs are those that change based on the level of activity. Just as businesses incur both fixed and variable costs, so too do consumers incur both fixed and variable costs. While certain costs are fixed in the short to medium term, in the long run, all costs for both businesses and consumers are variable. Businesses and consumers can change locations to reduce occupancy or shelter costs, vehicles and equipment can be sold or returned, etc.

For most consumers, their fixed costs are associated with their shelter (mortgage or rent payments), vehicle leases or finance payments, and periodic pension and personal insurance payments. In addition, certain utility charges consist of fixed or minimum charge as well as a component that is based on actual usage. While some consumers may consider payments on their outstanding credit card balances as fixed costs, in reality, maintaining unpaid credit card balances is a sign of poor financial health just as high blood pressure is an indication of poor physical health. Certain costs are typically variable in that they are generally considered to be necessities and vary according to usage. Consumer expenditures that fall into this category are food, utilities, gasoline and motor oil, public transportation, and other vehicle expenses. The majority of variable costs have both a variable component and a discretionary component. There is a portion of these expenditures that are truly discretionary in that we choose to consume a portion of them as an indulgence or psychological reward. For example, we might choose to consume filet mignon instead of hamburgers, eat at five-star restaurants rather than family eating establishments, drink eighteen-year-old single malt scotch rather than beer, etc. Expenditures that have both variable and discretionary components include food at home, housekeeping supplies, personal care products and services, reading, education, food away from home, alcoholic beverages, and consumer unit furnshings and equipment. Certain expenditures are discretionary in that they can be deferred for a period of time without impinging on our basic needs for food, shelter, and clothing. Consumers can delay purchasing the latest clothing fashions without suffering anything more than being considered out of vogue. Apparel and services, along with entertainment, have both a discretionary and a frivolous component. Purchasing expensive designer jeans for several hundreds of dollars or attending international film festivals would be, for most people, examples of frivolous expenditures. Because of the associated dangers to our health, expenditures on tobacco products and smoking supplies should be considered expenditures that should be avoided and allocated to other expenditures or ideally a source of savings.

Before one can satsify his/her financial obligations, most people will have to pay personal taxes on their income. As one goes from under thirty-five years to fifty-four years, one's personal taxes increase from 9.7 percent to 11.0 percent of his/her gross income. At retirement age, personal taxes consume less of one's income. Disposable income is what remains after personal taxes have been paid. Those under sixty-five years have between 89.8 and 90.3 percent of their gross income (pretax income) available to satisfy their financial obligations. Those sixty-five years and older have between 94.2 and 96.1 percent available.

Fixed obligations are as little as 24.9 percent of gross income for those consumer units headed by someone between forty-five and fifty-four years and subsequently increase to 34.4 percent for households headed by someone over seventy-four years. Fixed housing costs account for the majority of fixed financial obligations for all consumer units irresepective of the age of the head of consumer unit. It was as high as 59.6 percent in consumer units headed by someone between thirty-five and forty-four years and as low as 46.9 percent when the head of consumer unit was between sixty-five and seventy-four years. Fixed transportation costs range between 16.6 and 28.9 percent, depending on the age of the head of the consumer unit. As should not be a surprise to anyone, fixed health care costs increase with the age of the members of the consumer unit. The fixed health care of the youngest consumer units represent 5.2 percent of the unit's fixed costs while the costs for the oldest represent 24.3 percent. Other fixed costs represent between 5.4 and 11.2 percent of total fixed obligations. After accounting for fixed obligations, the amount of gross income available to cover remaining obligations ranges from 59.4 pecent of gross income for consumer units headed by someone less than thirty-five years to 64.1 percent for units headed by someone between forty-five and fifty-four years.

Variable obligations range from 31.8 to 45.6 percent of the consumer unit's gross income. Variable housing costs are between 30.2 percent and 34.9 percent of pretax income, food between 25.2 and 30.4 percent, transportation between 17.7 and 24.1 percent, health care between 4.1 and 14.5 percent, and other variable obligations between 7.2 and 12.0 percent. Those consumer units headed by someone sixty-five years or older devoted a higher percentage of their gross income to variable obligations than units headed by someone younger. As was the case with fixed obligations, consumer units whose head was between forty-five and fifty-four years devoted the lowest percentage, 31.2 percent of their gross income, to cover variable obligations. After taking into consideration its fixed and variable obligations, that same consumer unit had the greatest percentage of its gross income, 32.9 percent, available for other purposes. The consumer unit with least amount of its gross income available, 16.5 percent, was that which was headed by someone older than seventy-four years.

As was the case with the previously discussed financial obligations, the consumer unit whose head was between forty-five and fifty-four years devoted the least amount of its gross income on discretionary obligations at 10.8 percent. Both the younger and older consumer units devoted more. After accounting for all of their obligations, the consumer units headed by someone over seventy-four had incurred a deficit of 5.1 percent of their gross income, and those headed by someone between forty-five and fifty-four years a surplus of 22.2 percent.

CONSUMER INCOME STATEMENT							
		Age of Head of Consumer Unit					
		<35	35–44	45–54	55–64	65–74	>74
GROSS INCOME		**100.0%**	**100.0%**	**100.0%**	**100.0%**	**100.0%**	**100.0%**
Minus	**PERSONAL TAXES**	9.7%	10.2%	11.0%	10.2%	5.8%	3.9%
Equals	**DISPOSABLE INCOME**	**90.3%**	**89.8%**	**89.0%**	**89.8%**	**94.2%**	**96.1%**
Minus	**FIXED OBLIGATIONS**	**30.9%**	**28.0%**	**24.9%**	**26.0%**	**32.5%**	**34.4%**
	Housing	59.6%	59.6%	57.9%	52.9%	46.9%	53.8%
	Transportation	28.9%	26.9%	24.6%	26.5%	27.2%	16.6%
	Health care	5.2%	5.9%	6.9%	9.5%	18.2%	24.3%
	Other	6.3%	7.6%	10.6%	11.2%	7.7%	5.4%
Minus	**VARIABLE OBLIGATIONS**	**34.7%**	**31.8%**	**31.2%**	**32.8%**	**39.2%**	**45.6%**
	Housing	34.2%	33.7%	30.2%	32.0%	33.6%	34.9%
	Food	30.2%	30.4%	28.6%	26.8%	27.9%	25.2%
	Transportation	22.9%	23.1%	23.7%	24.1%	21.4%	17.7%
	Health care	4.1%	4.3%	5.6%	7.4%	10.0%	14.5%
	Other	8.6%	8.5%	12.0%	9.6%	7.2%	7.7%
Minus	**DISCRETIONARY OBLIGATIONS**	**11.4%**	**11.3%**	**10.8%**	**12.4%**	**13.3**	**21.3%**
	Entertainment	37.8%	41.1%	36.5%	31.1%	31.1%	38.2%
	Apparel and Services	32.3%	27.1%	25.3%	21.5%	20.9	10.6%
	Tobacco	5.1%	3.8%	3.8%	3.8%	5.2%	4.8%
	Other	24.8%	28.0%	34.4%	43.6%	42.8%	46.4%
Equals	**NET INCOME**	**13.3%**	**18.8%**	**22.2%**	**18.7%**	**9.2%**	**-5.1%**

Table 4-1 Realtionship between gross income and financial obligations expressed as a percentage of gross income.

Data: *2007 Bureau of Labor Statistics Consumer Expenditure Survey*

Souces of Gross Income

As we progress through life, our pretax or gross income will come from different sources. When we are young, the majority of our income will come from what we earn in our jobs. As we reach middle age, we are able to supplement our wages with income from other sources.

Finally, in our older years, we rely on sources of income other than wages. In 2007, consumer units headed by someone less than thirty-five years received 92.4 percent of their gross income from wages and salaries as well as self-employment income. In cases where the head of the consumer unit was over seventy-four years, these same sources of income accounted for only 15.9 percent of gross income. That same older consumer unit received 78.7 percent of its gross income from retirement and investment income. Government benefits, assistance programs, contributions, and other income sources accounted for between 1.4 percent in consumer units headed by somebody between sixty-five and seventy-four years and 2.1 percent of gross income in those whose head was less than thirty-five or older than seventy-four years.

SOURCES OF GROSS INCOME

| | Age of Head of Consumer Unit | | | | | |
	<35	35–44	45–54	55–64	65–74	>74
GROSS INCOME	**100.0%**	**100.0%**	**100.0%**	**100.0%**	**100.0%**	**100.0%**
Wages and Salaries	92.4%	91.3%	86.9%	76.0%	38.8%	15.9%
Self-employment Income	4.4%	4.6%	6.6%	6.3%	6.0%	3.3%
Retirement Income	0.5%	1.2%	2.9%	12.3%	47.4%	64.1%
Investment Income	0.7%	1.0%	1.8%	3.7%	6.4%	14.6%
Government Benefits	0.3%	0.3%	0.4%	0.4%	0.2%	0.9%
Assistance Programs	0.6%	0.6%	0.4%	0.5%	0.6%	0.6%
Contributions	0.7%	0.8%	0.7%	0.7%	0.3%	0.4%
Other income	0.5%	0.3%	0.2%	0.2%	0.3%	0.2%

Table 4-2   Sources of gross income by age of head of consumer unit.
Data: *2007 Bureau of Labor Statistics Consumer Expenditure Survey*

Personal Income Taxes

Most people have minimal control over their personal income taxes. That being said, it is still instructive to understand the kinds of personal income taxes one must pay and how those taxes differ depending on the age of the head of the consumer unit. In 2007, consumer units headed by someone between forty-five and fifty-four years paid the highest personal taxes, 11.0 percent of gross income, while consumer units headed by someone greater than seventy-four paid the lowest, 3.9 percent. The amount of federal income taxes and other taxes paid increased as a percentage of personal taxes with the age of the head of consumer unit. For those consumer units headed by someone less than thirty-five years, federal income taxes consumed 17.7 percent of their gross income and other taxes 1.7 percent. In consumer units headed by someone greater than seventy-four years, federal income taxes accounted for 40.1 percent of gross income and other taxes 16.8 percent. On the other hand, FICA, social security taxes, decreased with age from as high as 73.1 percent in consumer units whose head was less than thirty-five years to 31.4 percent in consumer units headed by someone greater than seventy-four years.

DISTRIBUTION OF PERSONAL INCOME TAXES						
	Age of Head of Consumer Unit					
	<35	35–44	45–54	55–64	65–74	>74
PERSONAL TAXES	**9.7%**	**10.2%**	**11.0%**	**10.2%**	**5.8%**	**3.9%**
Federal Income Taxes	17.7%	22.2%	28.2%	31.0%	36.0%	40.1%
State and Local Income Taxes	7.5%	7.2%	8.5%	7.6%	5.0%	11.7%
FICA	73.1%	68.2%	60.6%	57.3%	50.7%	31.4%
Other Taxes	1.7%	2.4%	2.7%	4.1%	8.3%	16.8%

Table 4-3 Distribution of personal taxes by age of head of consumer unit.
Data: *2007 Bureau of Labor Statistics Consumer Expenditure Survey*

Fixed Financial Obligations

Of the fixed financial obligations that the consumer unit must pay, housing costs, which consist of shelter expenses such as mortgage interest and charges, property taxes, maintenance, repairs, and insurance, accounted for the largest share in 2007. For renters, it was rental payments. Irrespective of the age of the head of the consumer unit, housing constituted the largest percentage of a consumer unit's fixed obligations. It ranged from 47.1 percent for consumer units whose head was between sixty-five and seventy-four years to 61.1 percent whose head was between thirty-five and forty-four years. Fixed transportation costs, which comprise vehicle purchase, finance, and insurance, accounted for as little as 15.9 percent of a consumer unit's fixed financial obligations to as much as 28.9 percent. Fixed health care costs are basically the premiums for health insurance, which are directly related to the age of the head of the consumer unit. The youngest consumer units devoted 5.2 percent of their fixed obligations to health care insurance whereas the oldest 23.2 percent. Life insurance and pension costs that together accounted for between 5.3 and 9.5 percent of the remaining fixed obligations.

DISTRIBUTION OF FIXED FINANCIAL OBLIGATIONS						
	Age of Head of Consumer Unit					
	<35	35–44	45–54	55–64	65–74	>74
FIXED OBLIGATIONS	**30.9%**	**27.3%**	**23.7%**	**24.6%**	**32.3%**	**36.0%**
Housing	**59.6%**	**61.1%**	**61.0%**	**55.8%**	**47.1%**	**51.4%**
Shelter	*100.0%*	*100.0%*	*100.0%*	*100.0%*	*100.0%*	*100.0%*
Transportation	**28.9%**	**27.5%**	**25.9%**	**27.9%**	**27.4%**	**15.9%**
Vehicles Purchases	*76.8%*	*72.7%*	*65.2%*	*68.5%*	*64.3%*	*65.5%*
Vehicle Finance Charges	*7.5%*	*6.9%*	*6.8%*	*6.7%*	*4.0%*	*2.3%*
Vehicle Insurance	*15.7%*	*20.4%*	*28.0%*	*24.8%*	*31.7%*	*32.2%*
Health care	**5.2%**	**6.1%**	**7.3%**	**10.0%**	**18.3%**	**23.2%**
Health Insurance	*100.0%*	*100.0%*	*100.0%*	*100.0%*	*100.0%*	*100.0%*
Other	**6.3%**	**5.3%**	**5.8%**	**6.3%**	**7.2%**	**9.5%**
Life and Other Insurance	*14.8%*	*17.5%*	*18.9%*	*22.4%*	*36.5%*	*46.6%*
Pensions	*85.2%*	*82.5%*	*81.1%*	*77.6%*	*63.5%*	*53.4%*

Table 4-4   Distribution of fixed financial obligations by age of head of consumer unit.
Data: *2007 Bureau of Labor Statistics Consumer Expenditure Survey*

Variable Financial Obligations

As was the case with fixed financial obligations, in 2007, housing consumed the highest percentage of variable costs across all consumer units. Natural gas, electricity, fuel oil and other fuels, telephone services, as well as water and other public services comprised between 45.1 and 54.8 percent of variable housing costs. Food consumed at home and away from home constituted the second highest percent of variable financial obligations. Food represented 25.2 percent of the variable obligations of consumer units headed by someone older than seventy-four years and 30.4 percent for units headed by someone between thirty-five and forty-four years. Food consumed at home consists of items such as cereals, bakery products, meats, poultry, fish, eggs, dairy products, nonalcoholic beverages, and fresh produce. All consumer units spent more on food at home than away from home. However, older consumer units tended to devote more of their food dollars to meals consumed at home than meals consumed away from home. Consumer units headed by someone older than seventy-four years allocated 64.7 percent of their food costs to meals eaten at home versus 53.5 percent for units headed by someone younger than thirty-five years. Variable transportation obligations consist of expenditures on gasoline, motor oil, maintenance, repairs, public transportation, and other costs. When a consumer unit's head is older than seventy-four years, there is a significant decrease in transportation costs. These obligations were 17.7 percent of variable obligations in consumer units whose head was over seventy-four years as compared to 24.1 percent in units whose head is between fifty-five and sixty-four years. As should not be a surprise to anyone, health care variable obligations, which include medical services, drugs, and medical supplies, increase with age. Consumer units headed by someone under thirty-five years devoted 4.1 percent of their variable expenditures to health care whereas units headed by someone over seventy-four years devoted over three times as much (14.5 percent as compared to 4.1 percent). Other variable financial obligations consist of alcoholic beverages, personal care products and services, reading, along with education. Those in their retirement years spent 7.2 to 7.7 percent of their variable expenditures on such items. Those consumer units headed by someone between forty-five and fifty-four years devoted much more (12.0 percent).

After accounting for their variable obligations, consumer units headed by someone over seventy-four years had 16.1 percent of their gross income available; those headed by someone between sixty-five years and seventy-four years, 22.5 percent; between fifty-five years and sixty-four years, 31.0 percent; between forty-five and fifty-four years, 32.9 percent; between thirty-five years and forty-four years, 30.0 percent; and less than thirty-five years, 24.7 percent.

DISTRIBUTION OF VARIABLE FINANCIAL OBLIGATIONS

	Age of Head of Consumer Unit					
	<35	35–44	45–54	55–64	65–74	>74
VARIABLE OBLIGATIONS	**34.7%**	31.8%	31.2%	32.8%	39.2%	45.6%
Housing	**34.2%**	**33.7%**	**30.2%**	**32.0%**	**33.6%**	**34.9%**
Utilities, fuels, and public services	*45.1%*	*47.9%*	*53.5%*	*50.3%*	*54.0%*	*54.8%*
Consumer unit operations	*17.3%*	*17.4%*	*11.4%*	*11.5%*	*11.4%*	*18.2%*
Housekeeping supplies	*7.7%*	*7.9%*	*9.6%*	*12.1%*	*10.5%*	*8.8%*
Consumer unit furnishings and equipment	*29.9%*	*26.8%*	*25.5%*	*26.1%*	*24.0%*	*18.3%*
Food	**30.2%**	**30.4%**	**28.6%**	**26.8%**	**27.9%**	**25.2%**
Food at home	*53.5%*	*55.8%*	*55.7%*	*55.4%*	*64.1%*	*64.7%*
Food away from home	*46.5%*	*44.2%*	*44.3%*	*44.6%*	*35.9%*	*35.3%*
Transportation	**22.9%**	**23.1%**	**23.7%**	**24.1%**	**21.4%**	**17.7%**
Gasoline and motor oil	*53.7%*	*51.1%*	*47.9%*	*44.7%*	*46.6%*	*39.6%*
Public transportation	*8.7%*	*9.6%*	*11.1%*	*13.6%*	*10.5%*	*21.7%*
Maintenance and repairs	*13.4%*	*14.4%*	*15.8%*	*15.8%*	*17.4%*	*14.6%*
Other vehicle expenses	*24.3%*	*24.8%*	*25.2%*	*25.9%*	*25.5%*	*24.1%*
Health care	**4.1%**	**4.3%**	**5.6%**	**7.4%**	**10.0%**	**14.5%**
Medical services	*67.6%*	*62.2%*	*54.9%*	*51.2%*	*45.3%*	*47.9%*
Drugs	*24.7%*	*28.9%*	*35.4%*	*39.1%*	*46.1%*	*43.6%*
Medical supplies	*7.8%*	*8.9%*	*9.6%*	*9.7%*	*8.5%*	*8.6%*
Other	**8.6%**	**8.5%**	**12.0%**	**9.6%**	**7.2%**	**7.7%**
Alcoholic beverages	*30.2%*	*22.8%*	*16.6%*	*23.7%*	*25.8%*	*19.0%*
Personal care products and services	*30.1%*	*32.2%*	*22.8%*	*28.2%*	*44.7%*	*39.4%*
Reading	*4.2%*	*5.2%*	*4.6%*	*6.7%*	*11.3%*	*11.9%*
Education	*35.5%*	*39.8%*	*56.1%*	*41.4%*	*18.3%*	*29.8%*

Table 4-5   Distribution of variable financial obligations by age of head of consumer unit.
Data: *2007 Bureau of Labor Statistics Consumer Expenditure Survey*

Discretionary Financial Obligations

Some may believe that the following financial obligations are not discretionary but necessities of life. However, as a means of properly managing one's financial health, minor changes to the following discretionary financial obligations can increase net income and consequently improve one's statement of financial condition. Entertainment consists of expenditures on fees, admissions, audio equipment, video equipment, pets, toys, hobbies, playground equipment, and miscellaneous supplies and services. In 2007, it accounted for as little as 31.1 percent of the discretionary obligations of consumer units headed by someone between fifty-five and seventy-four years and as much as 41.1 percent for units headed by someone between thirty-five years and forty-four years. Expenditures on fees and admissions at 20.3 percent of entertainment expenditures were lowest in consumer units headed by someone less than thirty-five years and highest at 27.2 percent in units headed by someone between thirty-five years and forty years. Consumer units headed by someone over seventy-four years devoted 30.8 percent of their entertainment expenditures to audio and visual equipment and services while units headed by someone less than thirty-five years devoted 42.0 percent. Pets, toys, hobbies, and playground equipment accounted for 16.3 percent of the oldest consumer unit entertainment expenditures and 23.9 percent of consumer units headed by someone between fifty-five and sixty-four. Other entertainment expenditures accounted for between 15.9 and 31.1 percent of discretionary financial obligations.

Expenditures on apparel and related services for men, boys, women, girls, children under twelve, footwear, and other products and apparel-related services are inversely related to the age of the head of the consumer unit. Consumer units whose head was greater than seventy-four years allocated 10.6 percent of their discretionary expenditures on apparel and related services while units whose head was under thirty-five years allocated over three times as much. Perhaps the most discretionary of discretionary financial obligations is tobacco. Not only did it account for 3.8 percent to 5.2 percent of discretionary obligations, but it also has been shown to adversely affect one's health. Stopping the use of tobacco products and smoking supplies will not only save money, but also reduce the possibility of incurring smoking-related diseases. Cash contributions were the most significant other discretionary obligations for all consumer units. They were directly related to the age of the consumer unit. The youngest devoted 63.6 percent of their other financial obligations to cash contributions whereas the oldest devoted 82.9 percent. Perhaps with the advent of age one becomes more charitable.

After accounting for discretionary obligations, consumer units headed by someone less than thirty-five years had net income of 13.3 percent of their gross income; by someone between thirty-five years and forty-four years, 18.8 percent; by someone between forty-five years and fifty-four years, 22.2 percent; by someone between fifty-five years and sixty-four years, 18.7 percent; by someone between sixty-five years and seventy-four years, 9.2 percent; and by someone older than seventy-four years, a net loss of 5.1 percent

DISTRIBUTION OF DISCRETIONARY FINANCIAL OBLIGATIONS

	Age of Head of Consumer Unit					
	<35	35–44	45–54	55–64	65–74	>74
Discretionary Obligations	**11.4%**	**11.3%**	**10.8%**	**12.4%**	**13.3%**	**21.3%**
Entertainment	**37.8%**	**41.1%**	**36.5%**	**31.1%**	**31.1%**	**38.2%**
Fees and admissions	20.3%	27.2%	26.0%	23.6%	22.9%	21.8%
Audio and visual equipment and services	42.0%	33.7%	35.6%	35.3%	35.3%	30.8%
Pets, toys, hobbies, and playground equipment	19.5%	20.6%	22.5%	23.9%	17.2%	16.3%
Other entertainment supplies, equipment, and services	18.2%	18.5%	15.9%	17.1%	24.6%	31.1%
Apparel and Services	**32.3%**	**27.1%**	**25.3%**	**21.5%**	**20.9%**	**10.6%**
Men and boys	24.1%	24.9%	23.5%	21.3%	19.3%	21.8%
Women and girls	34.6%	36.6%	43.5%	42.0%	48.1%	44.3%
Children under 2	9.8%	5.1%	2.5%	2.9%	2.4%	1.9%
Footwear	18.2%	17.1%	17.5%	18.6%	15.8%	14.5%
Other apparel products and services	13.3%	16.3%	13.1%	15.2%	14.4%	17.5%
Tobacco	**5.1%**	**3.8%**	**3.8%**	**3.8%**	**5.2%**	**4.8%**
Tobacco products and smoking supplies	100.0%	100.0%	100.0%	100.0%	100.0%	100.0%
Other	**24.8%**	**28.0%**	**34.4%**	**43.6%**	**42.8%**	**46.4%**
Cash contributions	63.6%	65.0%	66.2%	71.7%	71.0%	82.9%
Miscellaneous	36.4%	35.0%	33.8%	28.3%	29.0%	17.1%

Table 4-6   Distribution of discretionary financial obligations by age of head of consumer unit.
Data: *2007 Bureau of Labor Statistics Consumer Expenditure Survey*

Statement of Financial Condition

The statement of financial condition is a summary of the difference between what the consumer unit owns and owes. Should assets exceed obligations, then the consumer unit is said to have a positive net worth. Conversely, should obligations exceed assets, the consumer unit is said to have a negative net worth, a condition that could force the consumer unit into bankruptcy. While having assets that exceed financial obligations is nice, of far more importance is the extent to which those assets can be monetized. For certain assets such as cash, the value is clearly known and fixed. Other assets such as short-term investments, of which certificates of deposit and treasuries are examples, can be sold without significant risk of loss if liquidated prior to maturity. If held to maturity, there would be no loss.

Long-term financial assets, such as stocks and bonds, have liquid markets that establish prices at which investors are willing to purchase or sell them. It is nonfinancial assets that present the most difficulty in monetizing. Certain nonfinancial assets, such as cars, boats, airplanes, are relatively easy to value but can be difficult to sell especially in times of financial stress. If these items have been financed, the outstanding balances may exceed their realizable value at time of sale. Real estate, thought by many until recently to be an asset that only increases in value, has shown itself to be as exposed to market forces just as other asset classes are. By referring to comparable sales of similar homes in similar neighborhoods, one can get an approximation of the value of his/her property. However, one doesn't know until he/she actually consummates a sale, a process that can take months to complete and has high associated transaction costs, how much money will be realized. Just as most financial assets, houses are particularly subject to the strength of the local economy. Other nonfinancial assets, such as jewelry, art, coins, stamps, etc., may bring significantly less when sold than when they were purchased.

An examination of the current assets of consumer units in 2007 reveals that current assets tended to increase with the age of the head of consumer unit. Consumer units headed by someone under thirty-five years had current assets equal to 22.7 percent of their gross income while consumer units headed by someone over seventy-four years had current assets equal to 184.7 percent of their gross income. As a consumer unit ages, it needs to have an increased proportion of its assets available to satisfy unforeseen financial obligations. Long-term assets ranged from a nadir of 317.8 percent of gross income in consumer units whose head was under thirty-five years to an apex of 2,166.0 percent in consumer units whose head was between sixty-five and seventy-four years. The total assets of these consumer units ranged from 340.5 percent of gross income in consumer units headed by someone under thirty-five years to 2,286.1 percent in consumer units headed by someone between sixty-five and seventy-four years. To put these numbers into perspective, consumer units headed by someone under thirty-five years had total assets of $195.0 thousand; between thirty-five and forty-four years, $460.3 thousand; between forty-five and fifty-four years, $798.8 thousand; between fifty-five and seventy-four years, $1.1 million; and over seventy-four years $655.7 thousand.

Consumer units headed by someone between forty-five and fifty-four years had the least current obligations as a percent of their gross income (65.7 percent), and those headed by someone over seventy-four years had the highest (100.1 percent). Those same most senior consumer units had the lowest long-term obligations, 43.9 percent of gross income whereas consumer units headed by someone between thirty-five and forty-four years had the highest, 166.8 percent of gross income. Consumer unit net worth was 117.7 percent of gross income for consumer units headed by someone under thirty-five years and steadily increased to 2,054.8 percent in those headed by someone between sixty-five and seventy-four years.

STATEMENT OF FINANCIAL CONDITION						
	Age of Head of Consumer Unit					
	<35	35–44	45–54	55–64	65–74	>74
ASSETS						
CURRENT ASSETS	**22.7%**	**33.3%**	**57.4%**	**82.1%**	**120.0%**	**184.7%**
Cash	20.4%	28.2%	46.1%	60.0%	90.2%	101.6%
Short-Term Investments	2.3%	5.1%	11.3%	22.0%	29.8%	83.1%
LONG-TERM	**317.8%**	**568.1%**	**934.2%**	**1403.0%**	**2166.0%**	**1832.9%**
Financial Assets	17.0%	60.3%	141.6%	262.5%	505.2%	543.3%
Retirement Accounts	18.4%	60.5%	125.8%	233.1%	289.3%	97.5%
Nonfinancial Assets	282.4%	447.4%	666.8%	907.4%	1371.5%	1192.2%
TOTAL	**340.5%**	**601.4%**	**991.6%**	**1485.0%**	**2286.1%**	**2017.6%**
OBLIGATIONS						
CURRENT	**75.9%**	**70.0%**	**65.7%**	**69.9%**	**83.5%**	**100.1%**
Housing	30.3%	27.4%	23.8%	24.2%	28.4%	34.4%
Transportation	15.8%	13.8%	12.3%	13.5%	15.8%	12.6%
Food	10.5%	9.7%	8.9%	8.8%	11.0%	11.5%
Health Care	3.0%	3.0%	3.5%	4.9%	9.8%	15.0%
Apparel and Services	3.7%	3.1%	2.7%	2.7%	2.8%	2.3%
Entertainment	4.3%	4.6%	3.9%	3.8%	4.1%	8.1%
Other	8.3%	8.4%	10.5%	11.9%	11.7%	16.3%
LONG-TERM	**146.9%**	**166.8%**	**160.2%**	**151.4%**	**147.8%**	**43.9%**
Home-Secured Debt	115.3%	144.9%	139.0%	129.5%	126.8%	34.6%
Installment Loans	26.2%	14.9%	13.7%	12.9%	9.1%	2.3%
Credit Card Balances	4.3%	5.1%	5.5%	6.2%	6.5%	2.3%
Other Lines of Credit	0.2%	0.6%	0.5%	0.4%	2.9%	1.3%
Other Debt	0.8%	1.2%	1.4%	2.4%	2.6%	3.6%
TOTAL	**222.8%**	**236.8%**	**225.9%**	**221.2%**	**231.3%**	**144.0%**
NET WORTH	**117.7%**	**364.6%**	**765.7%**	**1263.8%**	**2054.8%**	**1873.6%**

Table 4-7   Realtionship between assets and financial obligations expressed as a percent of gross income by age of head of consumer unit.

Data: *2007 Bureau of Labor Statistics Consumer Expenditure Survey*
2007 Federal Reserve Survey Consumer Finances

Current Assets

Current assets consist of cash and short-term investments. The most liquid of current assets, cash, consists of checking accounts, savings accounts, and money market accounts. With interest rates at historic lows, there is no apparent advantage of trying to seek income on those balances that may be needed in the short term (thirty to ninety days). In 2007, cash accounted for as much as 89.7 percent of the current assets of consumer units headed by someone under thirty-five years to as little as 55.0 percent in consumer units whose head was over seventy-four years. All of the consumer units had their short investments in safe instruments, such as certificates of deposit and savings bonds, whose principal is backed by the United States government. In the event that these instruments are redeemed prior to maturity, there may be associated penalties that would reduce the amount realized. Therefore, the maturities of these instruments should be laddered so that early withdrawal penalties can be minimized. As a rule of thumb, certificate of deposit maturities should not exceed two years. Since savings bonds typically have longer maturities, they accounted for between 7.6 percent and 19.1 percent of the short-term investments. In reality, given their durations, they should be considered long-term assets. However, for consistency with the Federal Reserve's classification, they have been included as current assets.

DISTRIBUTION OF CONSUMER UNIT CURRENT ASSETS

	Age of Head of Consumer Unit					
	<35	35–44	45–54	55–64	65–74	>74
CURRENT ASSETS	**22.7%**	**33.3%**	**57.4%**	**82.1%**	**120.0%**	**184.7%**
Cash	89.7%	84.8%	80.4%	73.2%	75.2%	55.0%
Checking Accounts						
Savings Accounts }	100.0%	100.0%	100.0%	100.0%	100.0%	100.0%
Money Market Accounts						
Short-Term Investments	**10.3%**	**15.2%**	**19.6%**	**26.8%**	**24.8%**	**45.0%**
Certificates of Deposit	83.7%	80.9%	91.6%	89.9%	90.7%	92.4%
Savings Bonds	16.3%	19.1%	8.4%	10.1%	9.3%	7.6%

Table 4-8   Distribution of current assets as a percent of gross income by age of head of consumer unit.
Data: 2007 Federal Reserve Survey Consumer Finances

Long-Term Assets

Long-term assets consist of financial assets, retirement assets, and nonfinancial assets. Financial assets consist of bonds, stock-pooled investment funds, and cash-value life insurance, along with other managed and financial assets. Retirement assets are those that have been set aside for use during retirement. Nonfinancial assets consist of residential and noncommercial real estate, vehicles, business equity, and other nonfinancial assets. There are some interesting observations with regard to these three long-term asset classes. One being that irrespective of the age of the head of the consumer unit, retirement assets comprised the smallest percentage of the unit's long-term assets. Another, and even more disturbing, observation is that nonfinancial assets comprised a minimum of 63.3 percent of those consumer units' long-term assets.

Financial assets steadily increased from as little as 5.3 percent of long-term assets in consumer units headed by someone under thirty-five years to as much as 29.6 percent in consumer units whose head is over seventy-four years. Stocks and pooled investment funds comprised approximately 70 percent of the financial assets of consumer units headed by someone under seventy-four years. In consumer units headed by someone over seventy-four years, these assets comprised around 60 percent. As the age of the head of a consumer unit increase, so does that unit's reliance on other managed assets. Allocation of these other managed assets increased from 2.3 percent in the youngest of consumer units to 20.4 percent in the oldest.

Retirement assets as a portion of long-term assets increased steadily until the head of the consumer unit reached retirement age. Then, as one would logically conclude, these assets diminish during retirement. The key thing with respect to retirement assets is the need for liquidity, of known value, and availability to meet financial obligations during retirement.

Nonfinancial assets are ones whose useful life is measured in years. Some of them decline in value every year whereas others may increase or decrease depending on various unpredictable conditions. Vehicles, in general, lose one quarter of their value every year. Real estate, business equity, and other nonfinancial assets may gain or lose value over any period of time. The exposure to real estate ranged from 60.3 percent in consumer units headed by someone between fifty-five and sixty-four years to as much as 67.0 percent in those headed by someone over seventy-four. It is indeed unfortunate that those most in need of liquid income-producing assets have such a high exposure to such an illiquid assets class such as real estate.

DISTRIBUTION OF CONSUMER UNIT LONG-TERM ASSETS

	Age of Head of Consumer Unit					
	<35	35–44	45–54	55–64	65–74	>74
LONG-TERM ASSETS	**317.8%**	**568.1%**	**934.2%**	**1403.0%**	**2166.0%**	**1832.9%**
Financial Assets	**5.3%**	**10.6%**	**15.2%**	**18.7%**	**23.3%**	**29.6%**
Bonds	*3.5%*	*5.5%*	*10.6%*	*6.1%*	*8.0%*	*11.1%*
Stocks	*34.4%*	*33.9%*	*36.8%*	*30.9%*	*37.7%*	*41.9%*
Pooled Investment Funds	*35.6%*	*35.2%*	*30.3%*	*40.9%*	*30.5%*	*18.9%*
Cash-Value Life Insurance	*17.8%*	*9.1%*	*7.4%*	*6.3%*	*4.9%*	*5.3%*
Other Managed Assets	*2.3%*	*6.0%*	*11.1%*	*11.7%*	*15.0%*	*20.4%*
Other Financial Assets	*6.4%*	*10.2%*	*3.7%*	*4.1%*	*3.9%*	*2.5%*
Retirement Accounts	**5.8%**	**10.6%**	**13.5%**	**16.6%**	**13.4%**	**5.3%**
Nonfinancial Assets	**88.9%**	**78.7%**	**71.4%**	**64.7%**	**63.3%**	**88.9%**
Primary Residence	*58.7%*	*55.6%*	*48.3%*	*40.2%*	*45.0%*	*58.7%*
Other Residential Real Estate	*5.6%*	*11.0%*	*9.9%*	*12.5%*	*10.9%*	*5.6%*
Owned Vehicles	*9.2%*	*5.6%*	*4.2%*	*3.7%*	*3.4%*	*9.2%*
Net Equity in Nonresidential Real Estate	*2.7%*	*2.8%*	*4.8%*	*7.6%*	*7.3%*	*2.7%*
Business Equity	*22.7%*	*24.4%*	*31.1%*	*34.8%*	*31.4%*	*22.7%*
Other Nonfinancial Assets	*1.0%*	*0.5%*	*1.7%*	*1.2%*	*1.9%*	*1.0%*

Table 4-9 Distribution of long-term assets as a percent of gross income by age of head of consumer unit.
Data: *2007 Federal Reserve Survey Consumer Finances*

Current Obligations

There are several financial obligations that need to be satisfied on a monthly basis. These current obligations cover expenses associated with housing, transportation, food, entertainment, apparel and services, health care, and various other expenses. As the age of the consumer units reaches retirement age, there are increases in practically all current obligations. In fact, in consumer units headed by someone over seventy-four years, current obligations approximated gross income in 2007.

It should be of no surprise that the consumer units' largest asset, their house, is also their largest current obligation. Housing-related obligations were highest in consumer units headed by someone under thirty-five years at 30.3 percent of gross income and in units headed by someone over seventy-four years at 34.4 percent. The costs associated with the shelter component of housing (mortgage, insurance, and tax payments) accounted for over 60 percent of the housing obligations in consumer units headed by someone under fifty-five years. Since these costs are fixed, these are obligations for which consumer units should not overly stretch themselves. As the age of the head of the consumer unit increases, utilities (gas, water, electricity) become a more significant part of housing obligations, and furnishings and equipment become less significant.

Transportation costs are as low as 12.3 percent of gross income in consumer units headed by someone between forty-five and fifty-four years and as high as 15.8 percent in units with heads between sixty-five and seventy-four years. The combination of vehicle-purchasing costs and gasoline and motor oil, accounted for the most significant proportion of transportation obligations. Together they accounted for 55.0 percent of the transportation obligations of consumer units whose head was over seventy-four years and 70.0 percent in units whose head was less than thirty-four years. Vehicle insurance and the use of public transportation increased as the age of the head consumer unit increased. Their respective proportion of transportation obligations were 8.8 and 4.4 percent in the youngest consumer units, 14.6 and 13.9 percent in the older ones.

The proportion of gross income devoted to food-related obligations decreased from 10.5 percent in consumer units headed by someone less than thirty-five years to 8.8 percent in those whose head was between fifty-five and sixty-four years. In consumer units headed by someone older than sixty-five years, the proportion of food consumed at home increased from 55.4 percent of food obligations to 64.1 percent.

Surprisingly, consumer units devoted a higher percentage of their gross income to entertainment than to apparel and services irrespective of the age of the head of the consumer unit. Entertainment-related current obligations accounted for a minimum of 3.8 percent of gross income in consumer units whose head was between fifty-five and sixty-four years and a maximum of 8.1 percent in units whose head was over seventy-four years. Apparel—and services-related current obligations ranged from 2.3 percent of gross income in consumer units whose head was over seventy-four years to 3.7 percent in units headed by someone less than thirty-four years. Women's and girls' apparel along with footwear accounted for as little as 52.8 percent of gross income in consumer units headed by someone less than thirty-four years and as much as 63.9 percent in units headed by someone between sixty-five and seventy-four years.

As should be obvious, the amount of gross income required to satisfy current health care obligations increases proportionately to the age of the members of the consumer unit. The amount devoted to these obligations in consumer units headed by someone older than seventy-four years was five times that in units headed by someone less than thirty-four years (15.0 percent of gross income as opposed to 3.0 percent).

Other current obligations comprised between 8.3 percent of gross income in consumer units whose head was less than thirty-four years and 16.3 percent in units whose head was over seventy-four years. It is interesting to observe that irrespective of the age of the head of the consumer unit, cash contributions accounted for the highest percentage of these obligations. They ranged from as little as 21.6 percent in the youngest consumer units to as much as 50.4 percent in the oldest.

DISTRIBUTION OF CONSUMER UNIT CURRENT OBLIGATIONS

	Age of Head of Consumer Unit					
	<35	35–44	45–54	55–64	65–74	>74
CURRENT OBLIGATIONS						
Housing	**30.3%**	**27.4%**	**23.8%**	**24.2%**	**28.4%**	**34.4%**
Shelter	60.8%	60.9%	60.5%	56.7%	53.7%	53.8%
Utilities	17.7%	18.7%	21.1%	21.8%	25.0%	25.3%
Furnishings and Equipment	11.7%	10.5%	10.1%	11.3%	11.1%	8.4%
Operations	6.8%	6.8%	4.5%	5.0%	5.3%	8.4%
Supplies	3.0%	3.1%	3.8%	5.2%	4.9%	4.1%
Transportation	**15.8%**	**13.8%**	**12.3%**	**13.5%**	**15.8%**	**12.6%**
Vehicles Purchases	43.4%	39.6%	32.4%	34.8%	35.9%	29.6%
Gasoline and Motor Oil	27.0%	27.2%	28.6%	26.1%	24.8%	25.4%
Vehicle Insurance	8.8%	11.1%	13.9%	12.6%	17.6%	14.6%
Vehicle Maintenance and Repairs	6.7%	7.7%	9.5%	9.2%	9.2%	9.4%
Public Transportation	4.4%	5.1%	6.6%	7.9%	5.6%	13.9%
Vehicle Finance Charges	4.2%	3.8%	3.4%	3.4%	2.6%	1.1%
Other Vehicle Expenses	5.5%	5.5%	5.6%	5.9%	4.3%	6.0%
Food	**10.5%**	**9.7%**	**8.9%**	**8.8%**	**11.0%**	**11.5%**
At Home	53.5%	55.8%	55.7%	55.4%	64.1%	64.7%
Away from Home	46.5%	44.2%	44.3%	44.6%	35.9%	35.3%
Entertainment	**4.3%**	**4.6%**	**3.9%**	**3.8%**	**4.1%**	**8.1%**
Audio/Visual Equipment and Services	42.0%	33.7%	35.6%	35.3%	35.3%	30.8%
Fees and Admissions	20.3%	27.2%	26.0%	23.6%	22.9%	21.8%
Pets, Toys, Hobbies, and Playground Equipment	19.5%	20.6%	22.5%	23.9%	17.2%	16.3%
Other	18.2%	18.5%	15.9%	17.1%	24.6%	31.1%
Apparel and Services	**3.7%**	**3.1%**	**2.7%**	**2.7%**	**2.8%**	**2.3%**
Women and Girls	34.6%	36.6%	43.5%	42.0%	48.1%	44.3%
Men and Boys	24.1%	24.9%	23.5%	21.3%	19.3%	21.8%
Footwear	18.2%	17.1%	17.5%	18.6%	15.8%	14.5%
Children under 2	9.8%	5.1%	2.5%	2.9%	2.4%	1.9%
Other	13.3%	16.3%	13.1%	15.2%	14.4%	17.5%
Health Care	**3.0%**	**3.0%**	**3.5%**	**4.9%**	**9.8%**	**15.0%**
Health Insurance	52.7%	54.8%	49.7%	50.4%	60.2%	55.9%
Medical Services	31.9%	28.1%	27.7%	25.4%	18.0%	21.1%
Drugs	11.7%	13.1%	17.8%	19.4%	18.3%	19.2%
Medical Supplies	3.7%	4.0%	4.8%	4.8%	3.4%	3.8%
Other	**8.3%**	**8.4%**	**10.5%**	**11.9%**	**11.7%**	**16.3%**
Cash Contributions	21.6%	24.4%	23.3%	32.4%	34.5%	50.4%
Pensions	19.9%	20.9%	20.5%	18.9%	14.6%	6.1%
Education	12.7%	12.7%	20.0%	11.0%	4.4%	6.5%
Alcoholic Beverages	10.8%	7.3%	5.9%	6.3%	6.2%	4.1%
Personal Care Products and Services	10.8%	10.3%	8.1%	7.5%	10.8%	8.5%
Tobacco	7.0%	5.1%	3.9%	3.9%	5.9%	6.3%
Life and Other Personal Insurance	3.4%	4.4%	4.8%	5.4%	6.7%	5.3%
Reading	1.5%	1.7%	1.6%	1.8%	2.7%	2.6%
Miscellaneous	12.4%	13.1%	11.9%	12.8%	14.1%	10.4%

Table 4-10 Distribution of current obligations as a percent of gross income by age of head of consumer unit.
Data: *2007 Federal Reserve Survey Consumer Finances*

Long-Term Obligations

Mortgages or home equity loans comprise the highest proportion of home-secured debt. In 2007, they accounted for as little as 76.5 percent of home-secured debt in consumer units headed by someone between fifty-five and sixty-four years and as high as 91.6 percent in consumer units headed by someone less than thirty-five years. If one were to subtract home-secured debt from the value of residential real estate as shown in the long-term assets section of the statement of financial condition, one would discover that consumer units headed by someone less than seventy-four years had negative equity in their residential holdings of between 58.1 and 97.4 percent of their gross income. Only consumer units headed by someone older than seventy-four years had positive equity, which was 22.6 percent of gross income.

With the exception of consumer units whose head was less than thirty-four years, vehicle loans comprised the largest portion of installment loans. It ranged from 53.4 percent of installment loans to 88.8 percent. In those youngest consumer units, it was education loans that accounted for the most significant portion of installment loans, 53.1 percent.

In examining credit card balances, it is interesting to observe that the balances increased for all consumer units as the age of its head increased. Consumer units headed by someone less than thirty-four years had credit card balances equal to 4.3 percent of their gross income; between thirty-five and forty-four years, 5.1 percent; between forty-five and fifty-four years, 5.5 percent; between fifty-five and sixty-four years, 6.2 percent; and between sixty-five and seventy-four years, 6.5 percent. After seventy-four years, the outstanding balances decrease to 2.3 percent of gross income. This is in contrast to the increase in other debt of these same consumer units, which is 3.6 percent of gross income. It appears that other debt was being substituted for credit card balances in consumer units headed by someone over seventy-four years.

DISTRIBUTION OF CONSUMER UNIT LONG-TERM OBLIGATIONS

	<35	35–44	45–54	55–64	65–74	>74
			Age of Head of Consumer Unit			
LONG-TERM OBLIGATIONS	**146.9%**	**166.8%**	**160.2%**	**151.4%**	**147.8%**	**43.9%**
Home-Secured Debt	**115.3%**	**144.9%**	**139.0%**	**129.5%**	**126.8%**	**34.6%**
Mortgages or Home Equity Loans	*91.6%*	*85.8%*	*84.5%*	*76.5%*	*78.4%*	*78.4%*
Home-Equity Lines of Credit	*2.4%*	*2.7%*	*4.6%*	*5.8%*	*4.7%*	*11.9%*
Other Residential Real Estate Debt	*6.0%*	*11.6%*	*10.9%*	*17.7%*	*16.9%*	*9.7%*
Installment Loans	**26.2%**	**14.9%**	**13.7%**	**12.9%**	**9.1%**	**2.3%**
Vehicle Loans	*41.3%*	*57.7%*	*53.4%*	*53.8%*	*73.1%*	*88.8%*
Education Loans	*53.1%*	*24.4%*	*27.1%*	*21.7%*	*7.7%*	*8.2%*
Other	*5.7%*	*17.9%*	*19.5%*	*24.5%*	*19.2%*	*3.0%*
Credit Card Balances	**4.3%**	**5.1%**	**5.5%**	**6.2%**	**6.5%**	**2.3%**
Other Lines of Credit	**0.2%**	**0.6%**	**0.5%**	**0.4%**	**2.9%**	**1.3%**
Other Debt	**0.8%**	**1.2%**	**1.4%**	**2.4%**	**2.6%**	**3.6%**

Table 4-11 Distribution of long-term obligations as a percent of gross income by age of head of consumer unit
Data: *2007 Federal Reserve Survey Consumer Finances*

Opportunities for Improvement

There is nothing magic about improving your physical health or your financial health. A program of exercising regularly, maintaining the proper weight, and avoiding what is bad for you (tobacco, drugs, alcohol, etc.) are essential to enjoying a healthy life. With regard to your financial health, having a secure source of income, managing your financial obligations, and avoiding excessive debt are the basic ingredients for financial health. To put it another way, physiology is best when one burns off at least as many calories as one consumes; quaestrology is best when one spends less than one earns.

Income Statement

The income statement, a portrayal of the relationship between one's income and one's financial obligations, is the vehicle with which our quaestrological goals can be met. If one has money left over after satisfying his/her financial obligations, then one can build a positive net worth, the difference between one's assets and financial obligations. If, on the other hand, one's financial obligations exceed one's income, assets may have to be liquidated and/or debt may have to be incurred.

In examining the sources of consumer disposable income, certain factors may be fixed, which means they are beyond one's control in the short term and others are variable or discretionary, which also may or may not be controllable. The primary source of income for most consumer units is the wages and salaries that they receive. Unless one changes jobs or receives a raise, the only way to increase the wages and salaries of his/her consumer unit is for the earner(s) to work more. This may mean that the existing earners work additional hours or get a second job. It may also mean that other members of the consumer unit obtain employment. Social security and pension payments tend to be fixed although they may be indexed for inflation on a predetermined basis. Unemployment and workers' compensation as well as veterans' benefits also tend to be fixed.

Investment income is completely variable. How the consumer unit allocates its investments influences its investment income. Not having any investments means that there will be no investment income. Speculating or not diversifying one's investments may or may not produce any income and in extreme cases loss of principal. An in-depth discussion on how to make intelligent investment decisions is provided in the author's *A Common Sense Approach to Successful Investing, Utilizing the Power of Stratamentical Analysis*. Self-employment income is also variable in that income received is a function of the amount of effort expended. Support from others, gifts, and other sources of income are, for the most part, dependent on the actions of others over which the consumer unit may have limited influence and, therefore, have been classified as discretionary sources of income.

As we all know, taxes must be paid on our income. Federal and state and local income taxes along with pensions and social security payments as well as other miscellaneous taxes are subtracted from our income to give us disposable income, i.e., income that is available to satisfy our financial obligations. Our disposable income is a function of our fixed, variable, and discretionary sources of income after the appropriate taxes and other deductions have been taken.

SOURCES OF CONSUMER DISPOSABLE INCOME

	Fixed	Variable	Discretionary
INCOME			
Wages and Salaries	▨▨▨		
Social Security and Pensions	▨▨▨		
Unemployment and Workers' Compensation	▨▨▨		
Veterans' Benefits	▨▨▨		
Investment Income		▨▨▨	
Self-Employment Income		▨▨▨	
Support from Others			▨▨▨
Gifts			▨▨▨
Other Sources			▨▨▨
***Minus* TAXES**			
Federal Income		▨▨▨	
State and Local Income		▨▨▨	
Pensions and Social Security		▨▨▨	
Other		▨▨▨	
DISPOSABLE INCOME	▨▨▨▨▨▨▨▨▨		

Table 4-12   Classification of sources of income and taxes as to whether they are fixed, variable, or discretionary.

In managing one's income, the key to one's quaestrology is one's ability to manage one's fianancial obliagtions. To paraphrase a once-popular commercial, "It's not how much you make, it's how you spend it that counts." This does not mean that one must be a miser. It does mean that one must examine the consequences of the decisions that his/her consumer unit makes, i.e., how it allocates its income between expenditures, debts, and savings. Debt in itself is not necessarily bad. It is, however, bad when it is used to support a lifestyle that is not commensurate with the consumer unit's reasonable expectations for its income.

By committing to less-expensive long-term debt financed obligations, such as those for housing and vehicles, the consumer unit can reduce its finanical obligations without much suffering. A slightly smaller house that might have less amenities than one fantasizes over or a vehicle that doesn't have self-parking, voice-command systems, etc., may provide less ego satisfaction, but also may allow the owner to sleep better at night by not having to worry about how it will be paid for. Trading in the vehicle less often can also be a relatively painless way to reduce vehicle ownership–related transportation expenses. Once contractually committed to houses and vehicles, it is costly to get out of these obligations. The variable costs associated with housing and transportation can be reduced by performing more of the chores such as gardening, cleaning, washing, etc., rather than hiring someone to perform them is one way to reduce these variable costs. Another way is to purchase generic housekeeping supplies.

Health care also has fixed and variable components. Insurance, which constitutues the fixed health care component, can be reduced by ensuring that the benefits provided are consistent with the needs of the consumer unit. The variable health care costs consist of medical services, drugs, and medical supplies. Perhaps the best way to reduce these expenses is to live a healthy lifestyle thereby minimizing the need to incur these variable expenses. Not smoking, eating healthy foods, drinking alcoholic beverages in moderation, and exercising regularly not only reduce health care costs, but also can improve one's health. This is a practical "two for one special."

While food is a necessity of life, it is also one that can be easily managed. Consuming more meals at home and/or visiting expensive restaurants less often can reduce food-associated costs. Other ways include buying house brands as opposed to nationally advertised products, taking advantage of sales, using less-expensive cuts of meat, shopping at warehouse clubs and other discount merchants.

Apparel and related services represent discretionary rather than variable costs. Clothes and related items are constantly being outmoded with the change of seasons as designers and apparel companies constantly refresh their lines and change what is fashionable. If one is consumed with always being fashionable, one would obviously consider apparel not a discretionary item, but a mandatory expense. However, for those of us who are fashion insensitive, wearing last season's shirt, sweater, slacks, dress, etc., is not a big deal and is an easy source of savings. For those somewhat more fashion conscious, buying current fashions at the end of the season when they are on sale can also be a source of savings. Outlet stores, discount merchants, off-price merchants can also allow a consumer unit to reduce its apparel costs. The cost of children's clothing can be reduced by these same steps as well as taking advantage of hand-me-downs from relatives and friends. Footwear may be one of a woman's best friends, but really, how many pairs of shoes does a woman need?

All entertainment-related expenditures are discretionary. While we all need diversions from our daily travails, it does not mean that we need to be extravagant. We can go to concerts less often, watch sports on television rather than attending the event in person, delay upgrading our televisions to 3-D, wash our dogs rather than sending them to the groomer, or having our children play at the playground rather than having their own personal jungle gyms. These are just some of the many opportunities to reduce entertainment expenses without incurring any significant hardships.

Other expenses comprise fixed, variable, as well as discretionary components. Insurance and pension expenses tend to be fixed and are essential in providing protection for our families and security in our retirement years. Alocoholic beverages, personal care products and services, reading, and education have both variable and discretionary components. We could drink less alcoholic beverages or avoid premium-priced beverages. Personal care products and services expenses, while necessary to avoid being upresentable, can be reduced by using less-expensive products. Reading and educaion are important in that they are source of entertainment and allow us to acquire new skills. However, paperback books can be substituted for hardcover editions or even taken out from the library. Employer-sponsored educational opportunities should most definitely be taken adavantage of.

CONSUMER EXPENDITURES BY CLASSIFICATION

Expenditure	Fixed	Variable	Discretionary
HOUSING			
Shelter	▨		
Utilities, fuels, and public services		▨	
Housekeeping supplies		▨	
Consumer unit furnishings and equipment		▨	
TRANSPORTATION			
Vehicles purchases	▨		
Gasoline and motor oil		▨	
Public transportation		▨	
Other vehicle expenses		▨	
HEALTH CARE			
Health insurance	▨		
Medical services		▨	
Drugs		▨	
Medical supplies		▨	
FOOD			
Food at home		▨	
Food away from home		▨	
APPAREL and SERVICES			
Men and boys			▨
Women and girls			▨
Footwear			▨
Other apparel products and services			▨

85

CONSUMER EXPENDITURES BY CLASSIFICATION			
Expenditure	**Fixed**	**Variable**	**Discretionary**
ENTERTAINMENT			
Fees and admissions			▨
Audio and visual equipment and services			▨
Pets, toys, hobbies, and playground equipment			▨
Other entertainment supplies, equipment, and services			▨
OTHER			
Alcoholic beverages			▨
Personal care products and services			▨
Reading			▨
Education			▨
Tobacco products and smoking supplies			▨
Cash contributions			▨
Life and other personal insurance	▨		
Pensions	▨		
Miscellaneous		▨	

Table 4-13   Expenditures classified as to whether they are fixed, variable or discretionary.

Statement of Financial Condition

The statement of financial condition presents an inventory of the assets that a consumer unit has at its disposal and the financial obligations that it must satisfy if it is to be financially solvent. The extent that the consumer unit has prudently utilized its income is of major significance in the solvency of the consumer unit as measured by its statement of financial condition. The current and long-term assets as well as the current and long-term obligations present opportunities for improving the quaestrology of the consumer unit.

Current assets consist of cash and short-term investments. The purpose of having such assets is to provide a safety net of readily available funds that can be used when financial obligations exceed diposable income. As such, the emphasis must be on preservation of capital. Cash assets, as the name implies, are those that can be readily accessed when needed. Furthermore, there are no penalties associated with prematurely withdrawing these funds. However, this does not mean that there are not opportunities to earn some income without risking capital. While most banks do not offer interest-bearing checking accounts, some investment firms offer accounts that do pay interest on these accounts. They, like many banks, offer free checking accounts and online bill-payment services. While this may seem trivial, the ability to pay bills accounts online eliminates the cost of postage, which can easily represent a savings of five to ten dollars a month. Money market checking accounts are offered by many banks and other financial institutions. While these accounts have rarely inflicted losses on investors, there are no government-backed mechanisms, such as FDIC insurance, to protect money market account holders. In selecting a savings account, one does not need to restrict one's efforts to his/her local bank. Web sites such as Bankrate.com allow one to search for the most attractive rates on savings accounts and certificates of deposit irrespective of the bank's location. Short-term investments, such as certificates of deposit and savings bonds, are not nearly as liquid as cash. However, under normal conditions, they offer better returns than cash. With these instruments, there are often penalties for early withdrawal. In committing funds into these types of investment vehicles, one should ladder his/her money. Laddering is a technique for spreading one's money over different maturity dates so as to be able to take advantage of changes in interest rates and to have funds available to satisfy known future financial obligations, such as tuition payments.

Long-term assets consist of financial assets, retirement assets, and nonfinancial assets. The purpose of these assets is to provide a source of funds to be used at some time in a future that is measured in years. For most financial assets, such as bonds, stocks, and pooled investment funds, it is relatively easy to determine their value. For others, such as cash-value life insurance, other managed assets, and other finanical assets, determining their exact value at any given point in time requires more effort. The key point to remember about these financial assets is the importance of diversification, i.e., not concentrating funds in one asset class. As a general rule, stock investments have provided the best returns over extended periods of time. (For more details on the rates of returns of stocks and bonds refer to *A Common Sense Approach to Successful Investing, Utilizing the Power of Stratamentical Analysis.*) The purpose of investing in stocks is to provide returns in the form of dividends and capital appreciation. Whereas the purpose of bonds is to provide income. As the time these long-term assets are needed approaches, funds should be transferred to asset classes whose value will not be subject to the vagaries of the financial markets. While certain life insurance policies have a cash value, the main purpose of having these policies is to protect one's family should the policy holder die. With this in mind, one should examine the trade-offs between having life insurance with a cash value versus ones that offer more coverage for the same premium. Other managed assets and other financial assets are fine to have, assuming that the fees and lack of liquidity justify their existence in one's portfolio.

It is quite proper to segregate retirement assets in examining one's long-term assets. This is one area where all consumer units are underinvested. Retirement assets are meant to provide source of income during one's senior years. They should not be overly concentrated in one asset or asset class. One wants to avoid the tragedies of those Enron employees whose retirement assets were all invested in that company's stock. As rule of thumb, one should have no more than 20 percent of one's retirement assets invested in the company for which he/she works. (For more details on retirement savings, refer to *A Common Sense Road Map to Uncommon Wealth: The Key to Financial Success*.)

Nonfinancial assets basically fall into two categories, vehicles and real estate. Each of which are often acquired through loans of five, fifteen, or thirty years. Vehicles lose 25 percent of their value every year and, in the early years of ownership, have outstanding loan balances that exceed the value of the vehicle. Instead of trading in the vehicle when its loan has been paid off, one should keep it another year or more. While many supposed experts have espoused the notion that real estate only increases in value, the events of the last few years illustrate the fallacy of this notion. Not only have real estate prices not increased, they have actually decreased in many markets and, in some cases, quite signifcantly. To further compound the problem, the outstanding loans on many properties exceed the value of the underlying asset. Homeowners who stretched themselves and bought properties that they were unable to afford have been forced to face some very unpleasant choices. Furthermore, in most consumer units, their principal asset is their residence. The lesson here is quite simple, treat your residence as the place you live in and not the source of your wealth. Instead of stretching to purchase more houses, buy one with less amenities or smaller size. While keeping one's car longer and buying a less-expensive house reduces the value of one's nonfinancial assets, it also reduces one's financial obligations. The money saved can be used to increase one's financial assets.

The expenditures undertaken by the consumer unit as depicted in the consumer income statement manifest themselves in the current obligations of the statement of financial condition. Current obligations consist of housing, transportation, food, health care, apparel and services, entertainment, and other expenditures. The most significant current obligation is housing. Not only does housing represent a current obligation, it also has an associated mortgage that is the most significant long-term obligation for consumer units. The first and foremost way to reduce housing expenses is to buy a less-expensive home than you desire, but one that is still adequate to provide the location, space, and amenities that are consistent with your consumer unit's needs and not one that is more for ego satisfaction than as a comfortable home in which to raise a family. A less-expensive home means that there will be lower mortgage, insurance, and property tax payments. Keeping our homes a few degrees colder in the winter and a few degrees warmer in summer, shutting off lights in vacant rooms, using fans rather than air conditioners, and shutting off ventilation ducts in unused rooms can reduce utility bills without any incremental expenditures. Installing energy-efficient bulbs and appliances and adding insulation can reduce utility costs but make take several years to pay for themselves. Performing more household chores rather than hiring others to perform tasks such as gardening and cleaning the house and deferring purchases of furniture and other household items can also reduce housing-related obligations.

Transportation obligations can most easily be reduced by holding the consumer unit's vehicle after their loans have been paid off, purchasing a less prestigious vehicle, one with fewer amenities, and/or one that is more fuel efficient can significantly reduce transportation costs. Purchasing preowned vehicles can lower vehicle purchase prices but at the expense of higher maintenance and repair bills. Carpooling and utilizing more public transportation, where available, can also reduce transportation costs.

The importance of having adequate health care insurance cannot be overemphasized. This means having insurance coverage that meets the needs of the consumer unit. Policies with high deductibles may be appropriate for younger, generally healthy consumer units whereas policies with lower deductibles may be appropriate for older consumer units. Health savings accounts (HSA) may or may not be appropriate for a consumer unit, but it is one option to be considered in evaluating health care insurance policies. Certainly, younger consumer units may not need policies that cover colonoscopies while older consumer units may not need prenatal care. Most health insurance premiums are fixed for a year whereas other health care costs such as medical services, drugs, and medical supplies are based on usage. The old adage that an ounce of prevention is worth a pound of cure certainly applies in this case. Maintaining a healthy lifestyle along with preventive care and early treatment are the best ways to manage health care costs.

Expenditures on food are some of the more frequent purchasing decisions that the consumer unit makes. Daily, its members decide whether to eat a meal at home or away from home, drink an exotic beverage at the local Starbucks or a cup of machine coffee at work, eat a sandwich from home or an exotic meal at the bistro near work, etc. One or more times a week, most consumer units shop at the local grocery store whether it is at Whole Foods, Trader Joe's, or Kroger. Shopping at merchants that have a reputation for low prices rather than ones that are noted for the premium products they feature are opportunities for reducing food costs. Once you have the item in your home, can anyone discern the difference as to whether you purchased the Heinz ketchup on sale or at the regular price? Whether nationally advertised or generic private-label products are purchased can affect the costs of a consumer unit's food needs. Is there any meaningful difference in the taste? Eliminating one meal a month at multistar restaurants can also reduce expenditures on food. Will you really be depriving yourself by indulging in one less gastronomical experience?

What has been said about food expenditures is equally attributable to apparel, entertainment, and the other expenditures in the statement of financial condition. Certainly, we all need clothes, but are the clothes purchased at a Barneys that superior to the ones from a Macy's? When searching for opportunities to increase net worth, one of the more obvious means is to reduce expenditures in these categories.

Long-term obligations are the result of decisions that the consumer unit has made as to whether to pay for current expenditures with current income, short-term or long-term assets or through various forms of debt. Financing assets such as houses and vehicles, items whose useful life is measured in years, is an acceptable use of debt. Most of us have no choice but to utilize home-secured debt in order to purchase our home. In selecting a mortgage, one should take out fixed rate thirty-year mortgages when interest rates are at or below their long-term averages. Low rates will eventually be replaced by higher rates and sometimes significantly higher ones. If you can't afford the home at these rates, do not take out a variable interest rate loan that could possibly reset at a higher rate that you might not be able to afford. Do not count on appreciating home values that will allow you to refinance your mortgage and take out some equity. Your home is a place to live in not a piñata or a piggy bank that you can use to pay your bills. The time to consider variable rate mortgages is when mortgage rates are much higher than their long-term average. In evaluating variable rate mortgages or other forms of debt, it is important to take into consideration how often the rate will adjust and what is the benchmark that determines whether there will be a change. Some benchmarks are more volatile than others. In addition to fixed and variable rate mortgages, there are hybrids whose interest rate is fixed for a certain number of years but have a balloon payment at maturity. The problem with this type of loan is that you do not know what the prevailing interest rates will be at the time of refinancing and whether you will be able to satisfy prospective lenders' requirements. Home-equity lines of credit can be a useful source of funds in case of an emergency. Since the interest on them is tax deductible, they may be an attractive option to installment loans.

Installment loans may be necessary. However, in an ideal world, one would have set aside in advance the required funds in anticipation of these needs. Sometimes merchants, such as automobile dealers, appliance stores, etc., offer attractive terms that cannot be ignored. It is hard to not take advantage of 0.9 percent financing to purchase that vehicle that you really need, not the one that you have been fantasizing over. No interest, no payments for twelve months on appliances and the ilk can be attractive, if, and only if, you pay the entire balance off at the end of that time. If not, beware of the interest that has been accruing and turns this one-time bargain into a financial nightmare. Education loans are an investment in the intellectual capital of the consumer unit. The skills that are developed are critical in determining the earning capacity of the consumer unit.

Financing current consumption by maintaining outstanding credit card balance is not consistent with good quaestrology. Credit cards should be used as surrogates for cash or checks, not a means of long-term financing. To put it as bluntly as possible, if you are not going to have the funds available to pay outstanding credit card balances when they are due, don't make the purchase. Credit cards offering money back on purchases are preferable to ones offering airline miles or hotel stays. They are redeemable for money, which in the words of that great philosopher, Yogi Berra, "is almost as good as cash." Typically, these credit cards offer 1 percent back on purchases and sometimes have incentives of up to 5 percent on selected purchases such as gasoline. Frequently, you will receive inducements from credit card companies that offer low or even zero interest on balance transfers or checks that you can write against your credit card. In the fine print somewhere obscurely written is the caveat that there is a minimum fee of typically $10 or 5 percent of the amount transferred. If the balances are not paid off after the specified time period, the interest rate becomes significantly higher. As a general rule, beware of credit card companies offering checks or balance transfers.

After subtracting current and long-term obligations from the current and long-term assets of the consumer unit, we arrive at the consumer unit's net worth. Remember, it's not how many assets you have that is important, it is what those assets are worth based on their current market value after subtracting what is owed on them. If a house's realizable market value is less than its outstanding debt, the house is really a liability, not an asset, as many homeowners have unfortunately discovered. While house values generally have increased over long periods of time, the same cannot be said of that new car or boat that you bought. These assets typically lose 25 percent of their value very year. This means that after one year, that $20,000 vehicle is worth approximately $15,000; after two years, $11,250; after three years, $8,435; after four years, $6,330; etc. The value of other nonfinancial assets can only be determined at time of sale and should be valued conservatively when interpreting the statement of financial condition.

Quaestrological Summary

A quaestrological summary based on 2007 consumer data revealed some interesting findings. It should that the net worth of consumer units increased with the age of their heads. Consumer units whose head was under thirty-five years had a net worth of 1.2 times their gross income, a ratio that steadily increased to 20.5 times in consumer units whose head was between sixty-five and seventy-four years. An examination of the relationships between income and financial obligations reveals that consumer units headed by someone between forty-five and fifty-four years had the highest ratios of gross income to fixed, variable, and discretionary obligations (3.9 to 1, 3.4 to 1, and 9.3 to 1 respectively). Consumer units with heads between thirty-five and sixty-four years had the highest ratio of net income to gross income at 0.2.

Safety nets and long-term assets increased as the age of the consumer units' head increased. In consumer units headed by someone younger than thirty-five years, the safety nets were 0.2 times gross income and long-term assets were 3.2 times gross income. In the oldest consumer units, their respective ratios were 1.8 to 1 and 18.3 to one. In all consumer units, there was an overconcentration of nonfinancial assets. It was as high as 87.5 percent in consumer units whose head was under thirty-five years and as low as 63.1 percent with heads between sixty-five and seventy-four years.

Current ratios improved from 3.6 to 1 in consumer units whose head was under thirty-five years to 17.3 to 1 in ones whose head was between sixty-five and seventy-four years. The indebtedness and leverage ratios either remained relatively constant irrespective of the age of the head of the consumer unit or improved as the consumer unit head increased.

QUAESTROLOGICAL SUMMARY						
	Age of Head of Consumer Unit					
	<35	35–44	45–54	55–64	65–74	>74
NET WORTH	**1.2**	**3.6**	**7.7**	**12.6**	**20.5**	**18.7**
INCOME OBLIGATIONS						
• Fixed Obligations Coverage	3.1	3.5	3.9	3.7	3.0	2.9
• Variable Obligations Coverage	3.1	3.3	3.4	3.3	2.7	2.2
• Discretionary Obligations Coverage	8.8	8.9	9.3	8.1	7.5	4.7
• Income Surplus/(Deficit)	0.1	0.2	0.2	0.2	0.1	(0.1)
FINANCIAL CONDITION						
• **Safety Net**	0.2	0.3	0.6	0.8	1.2	1.8
• **Long-Term Assets**	3.2	5.7	9.3	14.0	21.7	18.3
Financial Assets	*0.2*	*0.6*	*1.4*	*2.6*	*5.1*	*5.4*
Nonfinancial Assets	*2.8*	*4.5*	*6.7*	*9.1*	*13.7*	*11.9*
Retirement Assets	*0.2*	*0.6*	*1.3*	*2.3*	*2.9*	*1.0*
RATIOS						
• **Liquidity Ratios**						
Current Ratio	*3.6*	*5.7*	*10.5*	*14.1*	*17.3*	*4.8*
Acid Test	*1.3*	*1.4*	*1.5*	*1.4*	*1.2*	*1.0*
• **Indebtedness Ratios**						
Debt Service Ratio	*0.2*	*0.2*	*0.1*	*0.1*	*0.1*	*0.0*
Financial Obligation Ratio	*0.2*	*0.2*	*0.2*	*0.1*	*0.2*	*0.1*
Consumer Debt Ratio	*0.1*	*0.1*	*0.1*	*0.1*	*0.1*	*0.1*
• **Leverage Ratios**						
Debt Equity Ratio	*0.8*	*0.4*	*0.2*	*0.1*	*0.1*	*0.0*
Debt Income Ratio	*1.5*	*2.2*	*2.2*	*1.8*	*1.2*	*0.2*

Table 4-14   Ratios summarizing the financial condition of the consumer unit segmented by age of head of household.

Data: *2007 Bureau of Labor Statistics Consumer Expenditure Survey*
2007 Federal Reserve Survey Consumer Finances

Profiles

As it is with most things in life, one size seldom fits all. While there are many ways to profile consumer units, the age of the head of the consumer units was chosen as the basis for the profiles presented in this chapter. Using the information already presented in this chapter, the reader can adjust the following profiles to account for the number of people in his/her consumer unit and their respective ages, housing tenure, region of the country, etc.

The following profiles show the actual and the desired range for the various elements that comprise the consumer income statement, the statement of financial condition, and the quaestrological summary. The numbers in these profiles are expressed as percentages of gross (pretax) income. In this way, the reader can simply multiply the percentages by his/her gross income to construct his/her own profiles.

Consumer Units Whose Head Is Under Thirty-five Years

In 2007, consumer units headed by someone under thirty-five years of age consisted of 2.8 people, one of which was under eighteen. The average age of the heads of these consumer units was 29.6 years. These consumers units had 1.5 earners and owned 1.6 vehicles. Of these consumer units, 46.0 percent were home owners and 54.0 percent were renters. Their net assets increased by 13.3 percent of their pretax income; at the same time, their net liabilities increased by 21.9 percent. This resulted in a decrease in their net worth of 8.6 percent of their pretax income.

Families such as these face several challenges. They have formed their families, assumed significant financial obligations, and must address the economic consequences of their actions. There are mortgages and car loans to pay off. Many have children whose education must be paid for in the future. If they are prudent in managing their finances, they can minimize the financial challenges that they may encounter later in life. First and foremost, these consumer units should eschew maintaining outstanding credit card balances. In addition, they should start building a safety net, an emergency fund, that can be used in the event of a financial setback such as loss of a job. While the heads of these consumer units are thirty or more years away from retirement, they should start saving for their retirement and take advantage of any employer-sponsored plans in which there are matching employer contributions. Unless income exceeds expenditures, it is obvioulsy impossible to amass the financial assets that might be needed in the future. To put it another way, unless you have something available to invest, it is impossible to achieve financial health

Consumer units whose head was under thirty-five years had gross income of $57.3 thousand in 2007. As with all consumer units, they should pursue any opportunities for increasing their income consistent with the quality of life that they choose. That being said, there are limited opportunities for reducing personal taxes. Reinvesting of investment income from interest and dividends should be looked at as a means of improving the consumer unit's wealth and not as something to support current lifestyles. In addition, there are relatively modest opportunities for reducing financial obligations that can provide signifcant savings that can be used to start building funds in anticipation of future needs. In terms of these consumer units' fixed obligations, buying a slightly less-expensive house and keeping cars a year longer can reduce their actual fixed obligations of 31.8 percent of their gross income to 29.2 percent. Eating out less often in addition to savings from having less-expensive homes can reduce variable obligations from 32.8 percent of gross income to between 28.8 and 32.2 percent of gross income. The most obvious category of discretionary obligations to reduce is tobacco, which not only can save money, but also minimize health problems that could occur later in life. Seeking less-expensive forms of entertainment and being more aggressive in pursuing bargains in apparel and other items can reduce actual discretionary expenditures from11.4 percent of gross income to a more desirable range of from 7.8 percent to 9.3 percent of gross income.

In 2007, the net income of these consumer units was 14.4 percent of gross income as compared to a desired range of 17.0 to 23.8 percent. Had the income from investments been reinvested, then there would have been an additional 0.7 percent of gross income that would have been available to produce additional income.

CONSUMER INCOME STATEMENT
Head of Consumer Unit Under Thirty-five Years

		Actual	Range	
	GROSS INCOME	100.0%	100.0% -	100.0%
Minus	PERSONAL TAXES	9.7%	9.7% -	9.7%
Minus	REINVESTMENT INVESTMENT INCOME	0.0%	0.7%	0.0%
Equals	DISPOSABLE INCOME	90.3%	89.7% -	90.3%
Minus	FIXED OBLIGATIONS	31.8%	29.2% -	31.8%
	Housing	58.0%	59.9% -	58.0%
	Transportation	30.9%	28.0% -	30.9%
	Health Care	5.0%	5.5% -	5.0%
	Other	6.1%	6.6% -	6.1%
Minus	VARIABLE OBLIGATIONS	32.8%	28.8% -	32.2%
	Housing	36.2%	35.5% -	36.8%
	Food	32.0%	33.0% -	31.0%
	Transportation	18.4%	18.1% -	19.2%
	Health Care	4.4%	5.0% -	4.5%
	Other	9.1%	8.4% -	8.5%
Minus	DISCRETIONARY OBLIGATIONS	11.4%	7.8% -	9.3%
	Entertainment	37.8%	32.1% -	36.6%
	Apparel and Services	32.3%	38.3% -	36.4%
	Tobacco	5.1%	0.0% -	0.0%
	Other	24.8%	29.6% -	27.0%
Equals	NET INCOME	14.4%	23.8% -	17.0%

Table. 4-15   Relationship between financial obligations and gross income.

An examination of the statement of financial condition for consumer units whose head is under thirty-five years reveals that their current assets at 22.7 percent of gross income are just barely above the target range of 19.2 percent to 57.5 percent of gross income. Furthermore, these consumer units have a disproportionate percent of their current assets in cash (89.7 percent) and the balance in short-term investments. By reducing their cash assets and increasing their short-term investments in line with the desired range, they can earn more money on their current assets. As is the case with current assets, their actual long-terms assets (317.8 percent of gross income) are at the bottom of the desired range of 318.9 percent to 489.4 percent. Both current obligations (75.9 percent of gross income) and long-term obligations (146.9 percent of gross income) exceed their respective desired ranges of 65.8 to 73.3 percent of gross income and 134.9 to 145.8 percent of gross income. The net result of all this is that these consumer units had a net worth of

117.7 percent of gross income as compared to a desired range of 118.2 to 270.3 percent.

STATEMENT OF FINANCIAL CONDITION Head of Consumer Unit Under Thirty-five Years				
	Actual	**Range**		
ASSETS				
CURRENT ASSETS	**22.7%**	**19.2%**	**-**	**57.5%**
Cash	89.7%	87.0%	-	36.2%
Short-Term Investments	10.3%	13.0%	-	63.8%
LONG-TERM	**317.8%**	**299.7%**	**-**	**431.9%**
Financial Assets	5.3%	9.0%	-	6.9%
Retirement Accounts	5.8%	2.5%	-	26.6%
Nonfinancial Assets	88.9%	88.5%	-	66.4%
TOTAL	**340.5%**	**318.9%**	**-**	**489.4%**
OBLIGATIONS				
CURRENT	**75.9%**	**65.8%**	**-**	**73.3%**
Housing	39.9%	42.1%	-	41.3%
Transportation	20.9%	20.3%	-	21.8%
Food	13.8%	14.4%	-	13.6%
Health Care	4.0%	4.6%	-	4.1%
Apparel and Services	4.8%	4.5%	-	4.6%
Entertainment	5.7%	3.8%	-	4.6%
Other	11.0%	10.2%	-	9.8%
LONG-TERM	**146.9%**	**134.9%**	**-**	**145.8%**
Home-Secured Debt	78.5%	81.2%	-	79.3%
Installment Loans	17.9%	16.8%	-	17.9%
Credit Card Balances	2.9%	1.6%	-	2.2%
Other Lines of Credit	0.1%	0.1%	-	0.1%
Other Debt	0.5%	0.3%	-	0.4%
TOTAL	**222.8%**	**200.7%**	**-**	**219.1%**
NET WORTH	**117.7%**	**118.2%**	**-**	**270.3%**

Table. 4-16   Relationship assets and financial obligations as compared to gross income.

The quaestrological summary for these consumer units reveals that with respect to all measures of their financial health, these consumer units are overextended. The capacity of their income to satisfy their obligations is at the lower ranges of the desired ratios of income to obligations. The ratios of their gross income to their financial obligations are also at the lower ranges of the desired ratios of income to obligations. Their current and long-term assets are barely sufficient to be considered within the normal range. Their other ratios, too, are barely at the minimal target ranges. These consumer units need to manage their finances so that they can decrease their expenditures relative to their income and devote the resulting savings into improving their financial condition. Increases in income, be they from raises, bonuses, overtime, etc., should be viewed as savings opportunities rather than excuses to splurge.

QUAESTROLOGICAL SUMMARY Head of Consumer Unit Under Thirty-five Years		
	Actual	Range
NET WORTH	1.2	1.2 - 1.7
INCOME OBLIGATIONS		
• Fixed Obligations Coverage	3.1	3.1 - 3.4
• Variable Obligations Coverage	3.1	3.1 - 3.5
• Discretionary Obligations Coverage	8.8	10.8 - 12.8
• Income Surplus/(Deficit)	0.1	0.2 - 0.2
FINANCIAL CONDITION		
• **Safety Net**	**0.2**	**0.2 - 0.6**
• **Long-TermAssets**	**3.2**	**3.0 - 4.3**
Financial Assets	*0.2*	*0.3 - 0.3*
Nonfinancial Assets	*2.8*	*2.7 - 2.9*
Retirement Assets	*0.2*	*0.1 - 1.2*
RATIOS		
• **Liquidity Ratios**		
Current Ratio	*3.6*	*3.5 - 9.4*
Acid Test	*1.3*	*1.4 - 1.5*
• **Indebtedness Ratios**		
Debt Service Ratio	*0.2*	*0.2 - 0.2*
Financial Obligation Ratio	*0.2*	*0.2 - 0.2*
Consumer Debt Ratio	*0.1*	*0.0 - 0.0*
• **Leverage Ratios**		
Debt Equity Ratio	*0.8*	*0.5 - 0.8*
Debt Income Ratio	*1.5*	*1.4 - 1.5*

Table. 4-17   Ratios summarizing the financial condition of the consumer unit.

Consumer Units Whose Head Is Thirty-five to Forty-four Years

The average age of the heads of consumer units whose head was between thirty-five and forty-four was 39.6 years. These consumer units consisted of 3.2 persons, of which 1.3 were under eighteen years. The 1.6 earners in these consumer units had annual income of $76.5

thousand in 2007. With respect to housing tenure, 68.0 percent were homeowners, of which 88.2 percent had mortgages on their homes. It is these consumer units who are potentially most vulnerable to endangering their finanical future. They have children to raise and educate along with mortgages and car loans to pay. This is no time in their lives to live beyond their financial means. If they have not already done so, they should redouble their efforts to prudently allocate their income between current and future needs. The increased financial obligations that they have incurred means that their safety nets must be even larger than consumer units whose head is under thirty-five years. These consumer units have fixed obligations of 28.7 percernt of their gross income as compared to a desired range of 24.7 to 26.5 percent, variable obligations of 29.9 percent as compared to 25.9 to 28.8 percent, and discretionary obligations of 11.3 percent as compared to 7.9 to 9.3 percent. While the most difficult to reduce, fixed obligations once incurred cannot be reduced until they are paid off and, therefore, should be incurred with caution. Variable obligations can be reduced with modest sacrifice and discretionary items with minor sacrifice. These consumer units have net income significantly below the desired range (19.8 percent versus 25.1 to 30.3 Percent). Reinvesting income from their investmenst would have represented an additional 1.0 percent that could have been used to produce future income. Unless these net income deficiencies are corrected in these households, it may be nearly impossible to achieve financial security as the consumer units age.

CONSUMER INCOME STATEMENT
Head of Consumer Unit Thirty-five to Forty-four Years

		Actual	Range		
	GROSS INCOME	100.0%	100.0%	-	100.0%
Minus	PERSONAL TAXES	10.2%	10.2%	-	10.2%
Minus	REINVESTMENT INVESTMENT INCOME	0.0%	1.0%	-	0.0%
Equals	DISPOSABLE INCOME	89.8%	88.8%	-	89.8%
Minus	FIXED OBLIGATIONS	28.7%	24.7%	-	26.5%
	Housing	16.7%	15.0%	-	15.8%
	Transportation	8.3%	5.9%	-	6.9%
	Health Care	1.7%	1.7%	-	1.7%
	Other	2.1%	2.1%	-	2.1%
Minus	VARIABLE OBLIGATIONS	29.9%	25.9%	-	28.8%
	Housing	10.7%	9.1%	-	10.6%
	Food	9.7%	8.8%	-	9.2%
	Transportation	5.5%	4.3%	-	5.1%
	Health Care	1.4%	1.4%	-	1.4%
	Other	2.7%	2.3%	-	2.5%
Minus	DISCRETIONARY OBLIGATIONS	11.3%	7.9%	-	9.3%
	Entertainment	41.1%	35.9%	-	39.9%
	Apparel and Services	27.1%	31.1%	-	29.9%
	Tobacco	3.8%	0.0%	-	0.0%
	Other	28.0%	33.0%	-	30.2%
Equals	NET INCOME	19.8%	30.3%	-	25.1%

Table. 4-18 Relationship between financial obligations and gross income.

The statement of financial condition of consumer units whose head is between thirty-five and forty-four years, reveals that they have insufficient assets and excessive financial obligations as compared to the target range for such consumer units. These consumer units are particularly vulnerable to overextended themselves financially. In previous generations, there were fewer multi-income families. In cases where there were multiple earners, it was often the case that the consumer unit would arrange their finances so as to live off the income of the primary earner and save the income of the secondary earner. Unfortunately, many contemporary consumer units must rely on the income of multiple earners to support their lifestyles. Even more unfortunate, as the statement of financial condition reveals, these consumer units have overextended themselves and exposed themselves to potential financial hardships should their consumer unit income stagnate or decline even slightly.

The current assets of these consumer units represent 33.3 percent of gross income versus a desired range of 41.7 to 71.1 percent and their long-term assets 568.1 percent of gross income versus a desired range of 613.7 to 864.0 percent. In times of low interest, the opportunity cost of having excessive cash balances is not significant. Nonetheless, prudent cash management would recommend minimizing cash balances in order to maximize income.

Of particular concern are the excessive nonfinancial assets that represent 78.7 percent of their long-term assets versus a target range of 46.4 to 66.3 percent. Since nonfinancial assets have dubious value, they may be difficult to monetize if funds are needed unexpectedly. Nonfinancial assets such as automobiles, boats, RVs, and the like can lose 25 percent of their value every year. Unfortunately, if they have been financed, as many are, the unpaid balances can exceed their market value. This is especially true during times of economic distress. Homeowners who believed that houses were an asset that only increases have been taught a hard lesson as many found themselves with mortgage payments they could not afford and outstanding balances on their loans that exceed the value of their homes.

Current obligations of 70.0 percent of gross income are above the desired range of 58.5 to 64.6 percent. Housing and transportation account for a significant portion of these obligations. Housing represents 39.1 percent of gross income and transportation 19.7 percent. Bearing in mind that they have a significant fixed cost component to them, they can become unaffordable if incomes become insufficient to pay for them. Since other current obligations, such as entertainment, food, apparel, and other items, vary with usage, they can be reduced by changes in priorities if necessary.

Long-term obligations of 166.8 percent of gross income exceed the desired range of 144.1 to 156.1 percent. Home-secured debt accounts for the vast majority of these obligations. While credit card balances and other lines of credit and debt account for a small proportion of long-term obligations, they are the easiest to reduce.

The net worth of these consumer units was 364.6 percent of gross income versus the target range of 452.8 to 714.5 percent. While having a net worth equal to 3.6 times one's gross annual income may seem like a satisfactory safety net, one should realize that a substantial portion of that net worth is in nonfinancial assets that may actually be significantly worth less than that shown in the statement of financial condition if forced to be liquidated.

STATEMENT OF FINANCIAL CONDITION
Head of Consumer Unit Thirty-five to Forty-four Years

	Actual	Range	
ASSETS			
CURRENT ASSETS	**33.3%**	**41.7%** -	**71.1%**
Cash	84.8%	40.0% -	29.3%
Short-Term Investments	15.2%	60.0% -	70.7%
LONG-TERM	**568.1%**	**613.7%** -	**864.0%**
Financial Assets	10.6%	9.7% -	7.0%
Retirement Accounts	10.6%	24.0% -	46.6%
Nonfinancial Assets	78.7%	66.3% -	46.4%
TOTAL	**601.4%**	**655.4%** -	**935.2%**
OBLIGATIONS			
CURRENT	**70.0%**	**58.5%** -	**64.6%**
Housing	39.1%	41.2% -	40.8%
Transportation	19.7%	17.5% -	18.5%
Food	13.8%	15.1% -	14.3%
Health Care	4.3%	5.2% -	4.7%
Apparel and Services	4.4%	4.2% -	4.3%
Entertainment	6.6%	4.8% -	5.8%
Other	12.0%	12.0% -	11.6%
LONG-TERM	**166.8%**	**144.1%** -	**156.1%**
Home-Secured Debt	86.9%	91.1% -	89.3%
Installment Loans	9.0%	7.7% -	8.5%
Credit Card Balances	3.1%	0.9% -	1.6%
Other Lines of Credit	0.3%	0.1% -	0.2%
Other Debt	0.7%	0.2% -	0.4%
TOTAL	**236.8%**	**202.6%** -	**220.7%**
NET WORTH	**364.6%**	**452.8%** -	**714.5%**

Table. 4-19   Relationship assets and financial obligations as compared to gross income.

As was the case with consumer units headed by someone younger than thirty-five years, the ability of consumer units whose head was between thirty-five and forty-four years to cover their financial obligations with their income was below the desired range in all categories of their quaestrological summary. In fact, their financial health was worse. Their liquidity, indebtedness, and leverage ratios all show these consumer units to be relatively illiquid and overindebted. Unless their deficiencies are corrected, they risk exposing themselves to potential future financial difficulties.

QUAESTROLOGICAL SUMMARY			
Head of Consumer Unit Thirty-five to Forty-four Years			
	Actual	**Range**	
NET WORTH	3.6	4.5 -	7.1
INCOME OBLIGATIONS			
• Fixed Obligations Coverage	3.5	3.8 -	4.0
• Variable Obligations Coverage	3.3	3.5 -	3.9
• Discretionary Obligations Coverage	8.9	10.7 -	12.7
• Income Surplus (Deficit)	0.2	0.3 -	0.3
FINANCIAL CONDITION			
• **Safety Net**	**0.3**	**0.4** -	**0.7**
• **Long-TermAssets**	**5.7**	**6.1** -	**8.6**
Financial Assets	*0.6*	*0.6* -	*0.6*
Nonfinancial Assets	*4.5*	*4.0* -	*4.1*
Retirement Assets	*0.6*	*1.5* -	*4.0*
RATIOS			
• **Liquidity Ratios**			
Current Ratio	*5.7*	*8.5* -	*13.2*
Acid Test	*1.4*	*1.5* -	*1.7*
• **Indebtedness Ratios**			
Debt Service Ratio	*0.2*	*0.1* -	*0.1*
Financial Obligation Ratio	*0.2*	*0.2* -	*0.2*
Consumer Debt Ratio	*0.1*	*0.0* -	*0.0*
• **Leverage Ratios**			
Debt Equity Ratio	*0.4*	*0.2* -	*0.3*
Debt Income Ratio	*2.2*	*2.0* -	*2.1*

Table. 4-20   Ratios summarizing the financial condition of the consumer unit.

Consumer Units Whose Head Is Forty-five to Fifty-four Years

In 2007, the average age of the head of consumer units whose head was between forty-five and fifty-four years was 49.4. These households consisted of 2.7 people, of which 0.6 were under eighteen years. They had 1.7 earners, which is larger than that of any consumer unit irrespective of the age of its head. With respective to housing tenure, 75.0 percent of these consumer units were homeowners, of which 78.7 percent had outstanding mortgages. The annual gross income of these households was $80.6 thousand, an amount that exceeds that of any other consumer units. Even though the temptation may be great, this is no time for the consumer unit to increase its fixed financial obligations as they may be unaffordable as income in later years may be significantly reduced.

The amount of these consumer units' income devoted to satsisfying their financial obligations exceeded the target range. Actual fixed obligations were 25.6 percent of gross income as compared to a target range of 21.5 to 23.0 percent; variable obligations, 29.3 percent versus 25.2 to 27.9 percent; and discretionary obligations, 10.8 percent versus 7.6 to 9.0 percent. As a result, their net income was 23.3 percent of gross income as opposed to a target range of 29.1 to 32.9 percent. Income from investments represented 1.8 percent of gross income, an amount that could have been reinvested.

CONSUMER INCOME STATEMENT
Head of Consumer Unit Forty-five to Fifty Four Years

		Actual	Range	
	GROSS INCOME	**100.0%**	**100.0%**	**100.0%**
Minus	**PERSONAL TAXES**	**11.0%**	**11.0%** -	**11.0%**
Minus	**REINVESTMENT INVESTMENT INCOME**	**0.0%**	**1.8%** -	**0.0%**
Equals	**DISPOSABLE INCOME**	**89.0%**	**87.2%** -	**89.0%**
Minus	**FIXED OBLIGATIONS**	**25.6%**	**21.5%** -	**23.0%**
	Housing	14.4%	12.3% -	13.0%
	Transportation	6.8%	4.9% -	5.7%
	Health Care	1.7%	1.7% -	1.7%
	Other	2.6%	2.6% -	2.6%
Minus	**VARIABLE OBLIGATIONS**	**29.3%**	**25.2%** -	**27.9%**
	Housing	9.4%	7.6% -	8.9%
	Food	8.9%	8.1% -	8.5%
	Transportation	5.5%	4.4% -	5.1%
	Health Care	1.7%	1.7% -	1.7%
	Other	3.7%	3.3% -	3.6%
Minus	**DISCRETIONARY OBLIGATIONS**	**10.8%**	**7.6%** -	**9.0%**
	Entertainment	36.5%	31.0% -	35.1%
	Apparel and Services	25.3%	28.7% -	27.8%
	Tobacco	3.8%	0.0% -	0.0%
	Other	34.4%	40.2% -	37.1%
Equals	**NET INCOME**	**23.3%**	**32.9%** -	**29.1%**

Table. 4-21　Relationship between financial obligations and gross income.

In consumer units headed by someone between forty-five and fifty-four years, both current and long-term assets are within the desired ranges, albeit at the lower end of the ranges. Current assets of 57.4 percent of gross income compare favorably to a desired range of 41.7 to 88.4 percent and long-term assets of 934.2 percent to 873.2 to 2,032.7

percent. With respect to current assets, these consumer units have a higher concentration of their assets in cash as opposed to short-term investments than the target ranges. Unfortunately, these consumer units are overextended. Their current and long-term financial obligations exceed the desired range. The target range for current obligations is 54.3 to 59.9 percent of gross income whereas the actual amount was 65.7 percent. With respect to long-term obligations, the desired range is 129.6 to 1,41.4 percent of gross income as compared to the actual 160.2 percent. Despite their excessive financial obligations, their net worth of 765.7 percent of gross income is at the lower portion of the target range of 730.9 to 1,919.8 percent.

STATEMENT OF FINANCIAL CONDITION
Head of Consumer Unit Forty-five to Fifty-four Years

	Actual	Range		
ASSETS				
CURRENT ASSETS	**57.4%**	**41.7%**	**-**	**88.4%**
Cash	80.4%	40.0%	-	23.6%
Short-Term Investments	19.6%	60.0%	-	76.4%
LONG-TERM	**934.2%**	**873.2%**	**-**	**2032.7%**
Financial Assets	15.2%	11.6%	-	5.0%
Retirement Accounts	13.5%	20.3%	-	66.5%
Nonfinancial Assets	71.4%	68.1%	-	28.5%
TOTAL	**991.6%**	**914.9%**	**-**	**2121.1%**
OBLIGATIONS				
CURRENT	**65.7%**	**54.3%**	**-**	**59.9%**
Housing	36.3%	36.5%	-	36.6%
Transportation	18.8%	17.1%	-	18.1%
Food	13.6%	15.0%	-	14.2%
Health Care	5.3%	6.4%	-	5.8%
Apparel and Services	4.1%	4.0%	-	4.2%
Entertainment	6.0%	4.4%	-	5.3%
Other	16.0%	16.7%	-	15.9%
LONG-TERM	**160.2%**	**129.6%**	**-**	**141.4%**
Home-Secured Debt	86.8%	92.3%	-	90.1%
Installment Loans	8.6%	7.7%	-	8.6%
Credit Card Balances	3.4%	0.0%	-	1.0%
Other Lines of Credit	0.3%	0.0%	-	0.1%
Other Debt	0.9%	0.0%	-	0.3%
TOTAL	**225.9%**	**184.0%**	**-**	**201.2%**
NET WORTH	**765.7%**	**730.9%**	**-**	**1919.8%**

Table. 4-22   Relationship assets and financial obligations as compared to gross income.

The quaestrological summary for these consumer units reveals that their ability to satisfy their fixed, variable, and discretionary obligations is below the desired ranges. While both their current (safety net) and long-term assets are within the target ranges, their nonfinancial assets of 6.7 times gross income exceed the desired range of 5.8 to 5.9 times and their retirement assets of 1.3 times are below the 1.8 to 13.5 times range. While certain ratios such as the current ratio and safety net are within expectations, others such as the acid test, retirement coverage, financial obligation ratio, and the debt income ratio are not within their respective desired ranges.

QUAESTROLOGICAL SUMMARY Head of Consumer Unit Forty-five to Fifty-four Years				
	Actual	**Range**		
NET WORTH	7.7	7.3	-	19.2
INCOME OBLIGATIONS				
• Fixed Obligations Coverage	3.9	4.3	-	4.7
• Variable Obligations Coverage	3.4	3.6	-	4.0
• Discretionary Obligations Coverage	9.3	11.2	-	13.1
• Income Surplus (Deficit)	0.2	0.3	-	0.3
FINANCIAL CONDITION				
• **Safety Net**	**0.6**	**0.4**	**-**	**0.9**
• **Long-TermAssets**	**9.3**	**8.7**	**-**	**20.3**
Financial Assets	*1.4*	*1.0*	*-*	*1.0*
Nonfinancial Assets	*6.7*	*5.9*	*-*	*5.9*
Retirement Assets	*1.3*	*1.8*	*-*	*13.5*
RATIOS				
• **Liquidity Ratios**				
Current Ratio	*10.5*	*9.2*	*-*	*17.7*
Acid Test	*1.5*	*1.7*	*-*	*1.8*
• **Indebtedness Ratios**				
Debt Service Ratio	*0.1*	*0.1*	*-*	*0.1*
Financial Obligation Ratio	*0.2*	*0.1*	*-*	*0.1*
Consumer Debt Ratio	*0.1*	*0.0*	*-*	*0.0*
• **Leverage Ratios**				
Debt Equity Ratio	*0.2*	*0.1*	*-*	*0.2*
Debt Income Ratio	*2.2*	*1.9*	*-*	*2.0*

Table. 4-23   Ratios summarizing the financial condition of the consumer unit.

Consumer Units Whose Head Is Fifty-five to Sixty-four Years

Consumer units headed by someone between fifty-five and sixty-four years had annual gross income of $71.0 thousand, an amount that represents a 11.9 percent decrease from that of consumer units headed by someone between forty-five and fifty-four years. These consumer units had 2.1 members, of which only 0.2 were under eighteen years, and 1.4 were wage earners. Of these households, 81.0 percent were homeowners, of which 58.0 percent had outstanding mortgages on their homes. The avergae age of the heads of these consumer units was 59.2 years.

The ramifications of the decrease in their gross income is very simple. While certain obligations, such as educating their children, have been reduced, these households should not view this as an opportunity to indulge themselves in extravagances. Purchases of second homes, expensive cars, boats, and RVs should be undertaken with caution. Servicing those fixed financial obligations may not be possible as consumer unit income tends to shrink as the consumer unit ages and is no longer able to work full-time. Of course, if these consumer units have substantial financial assets and their retirement assets are sufficient to sustain them through their later years, then they should reward themselves.

These consumer units are more exposed to two threats to their quaestrology than younger consumer units. One is being unemployed, and the other is becoming disabled. Workers in their preretirement years are often more susceptible to losing their jobs than younger ones. Furthermore, should they be unfortunate to lose their jobs, many will find it more difficult, if not impossible, to find new employment than younger workers. Many may be forced to accept lower salaries than they were accustomed to. As one ages, one becomes more susceptible to deteriorating health that may render the individual unable to continue working. In addition to having adequate health insurance, disability insurance and long-term care insurance can help mitigate their finanical impact on the household.

The fixed obligations of these consumer units of 26.8 percent of gross income exceed the desired range of 21.3 to 23.4 percent. As with all consumer units, housing and transportation account for more than three-quarters of fixed obligations. Since these obligations may extend from three to five years for transportation-related fixed costs and as much as thirty years for houses, these consumer units should satisfy themselves that they will have sufficient income to satisfy these obligations during their retirement years. The variable obligations of 30.7 percent of gross income exceed the desired range of 27.7 to 29.0 percent. A commensurate decrease in housing and transportation variable costs can be achieved by reducing their fixed costs. In addition, consuming fewer meals away from home and more aggressively purchasing discounted items can reduce food costs, which are the second largest component of variable obligations. The normal range for discretionary obligations is 9.1 to 10.4 percent of consumer unit annual gross income, which is significantly lower than the actual 12.4 percent of these consumer units. It is really up to each of these consumer units as to how they will incur discretionary obligations. Deferring purchases on desired but not essential items can provide additional income that can be saved for retirement.

In 2007, consumer units whose head was between fifty-five and sixty-four had 20.0 percent of their gross income remaining after satisfying their financial obligations. However, this is far below the target range of 27.0 to 29.0 percent. Had investment income been reinvested, 3.7 percent of gross income would have been available to provide additional income in the future.

		Actual	Range	
CONSUMER INCOME STATEMENT Head of Consumer Unit Fifty-five to Sixty-four Years				
GROSS INCOME		100.0%	100.0%	100.0%
Minus	**PERSONAL TAXES**	10.2%	10.2% - 10.2%	
Minus	**REINVESTMENT INVESTMENT INCOME**	0.0%	3.7% - 0.0%	
Equals	**DISPOSABLE INCOME**	89.8%	86.1% - 89.8%	
Minus	**FIXED OBLIGATIONS**	26.8%	21.3% - 23.4%	
	Housing	13.7%	51.7% - 11.7%	
	Transportation	7.7%	23.1% - 6.4%	
	Health Care	2.5%	11.6% - 2.5%	
	Other	2.9%	13.6% - 2.9%	
Minus	**VARIABLE OBLIGATIONS**	30.7%	27.7% - 29.0%	
	Housing	10.5%	30.3% - 9.7%	
	Food	8.8%	28.9% - 8.4%	
	Transportation	5.8%	22.3% - 5.5%	
	Health Care	2.4%	8.8% - 2.4%	
	Other	3.2%	9.7% - 3.0%	
Minus	**DISCRETIONARY OBLIGATIONS**	12.4%	9.1% - 10.4%	
	Entertainment	31.1%	25.2% - 29.4%	
	Apparel and Services	21.5%	23.7% - 23.3%	
	Tobacco	3.8%	0.0% - 0.0%	
	Other	43.6%	51.1% - 47.3%	
Equals	**NET INCOME**	20.0%	29.0% - 27.0%	

Table. 4-24   Relationship between financial obligations and gross income.

Consumer units whose head is between fifty-five and sixty-four years need to be especially concerned with their statements of financial condition as this will be a critical component in determining their quaestrology during their retirement years. While current assets of 82.1 percent of gross income are well within the desired range of 41.7 to 114.4 percent, the same cannot be said for long-term assets, which at 1,403.0 percent of gross income are significantly below the desired range of 3,128.0 to 5,196.2 percent. These consumer units are overexposed to nonfinancial assets, which account for 64.7 percent of their long-term assets as compared to the target range of 14.9 to 24.8 percent. As stated previously, it can be difficult to liquidate nonfinancial assets such as houses, boats, cars, etc. Both current obligations of 69.9 percent of gross income and long-term obligations of 151.4 percent exceed their respective target ranges of 57.1 to 62.9 percent and 115.0 and 127.2 percent. As a result of these disparities between actual assets and obligations and their respective ranges, the net worth of these consumer units was 1,263.8 percent of gross income as compared to a desired range of 3,087.5 to 5,120.6 percent.

STATEMENT OF FINANCIAL CONDITION
Head of Consumer Unit Fifty-five to Sixty-four Years

	Actual	Range	
ASSETS			
CURRENT ASSETS	**82.1%**	**41.7%** -	**114.4%**
Cash	73.2%	40.0% -	18.2%
Short-Term Investments	26.8%	60.0% -	81.8%
LONG-TERM	**1403.0%**	**3218.0%** -	**5196.2%**
Financial Assets	18.7%	5.9% -	3.7%
Retirement Accounts	16.6%	69.3% -	81.4%
Nonfinancial Assets	64.7%	24.8% -	14.9%
TOTAL	**1485.0%**	**3259.6%** -	**5310.6%**
OBLIGATIONS			
CURRENT	**69.9%**	**57.1%** -	**62.9%**
Housing	34.7%	33.9% -	34.0%
Transportation	19.4%	17.9% -	18.9%
Food	12.6%	14.0% -	13.4%
Health Care	7.0%	8.6% -	7.8%
Apparel and Services	3.8%	3.8% -	3.9%
Entertainment	5.5%	4.0% -	4.9%
Other	17.1%	17.9% -	17.2%
LONG-TERM	**151.4%**	**115.0%** -	**127.2%**
Home-Secured Debt	85.6%	93.1% -	90.2%
Installment Loans	8.5%	6.9% -	8.1%
Credit Card Balances	4.1%	0.0% -	1.2%
Other Lines of Credit	0.3%	0.0% -	0.1%
Other Debt	1.6%	0.0% -	0.5%
TOTAL	**221.2%**	**172.1%** -	**190.0%**
NET WORTH	**1263.8%**	**3087.5%** -	**5120.6%**

Table. 4-25   Relationship assets and financial obligations as compared to gross income.

While there are significant variances between actual and target range measures of the various elements of the quaestrological summary for these consumer units, the most significant is the relationship between the actual retirement coverage ratio of 2.3 times annual gross income and the desired range of 22.3 to 42.3 times annual gross income. With retirement looming in a few years, these consumer units face a challenging retirement. They must hope that their health allows them to continue working longer, or it might be necessary to reduce their standard of living.

QUAESTROLOGICAL SUMMARY
Head of Consumer Unit Fifty-five to Sixty-four Years

	Actual	Range
NET WORTH	12.6	30.9 - 51.2
INCOME OBLIGATIONS		
• Fixed Obligations Coverage	3.7	4.3 - 4.6
• Variable Obligations Coverage	3.3	3.5 - 3.8
• Discretionary Obligations Coverage	8.1	9.6 - 11.0
• Income Surplus (Deficit)	0.2	0.3 - 0.3
FINANCIAL CONDITION		
• **Safety Net**	**0.8**	**0.4 - 1.1**
• **Long-Term Assets**	**14.0**	**32.2 - 52.0**
Financial Assets	*2.6*	*1.9 - 1.9*
Nonfinancial Assets	*9.1*	*7.8 - 8.0*
Retirement Assets	*2.3*	*22.3 - 42.3*
RATIOS		
• **Liquidity Ratios**		
Current Ratio	*14.1*	*8.8 - 21.8*
Acid Test	*1.4*	*1.6 - 1.8*
• **Indebtedness Ratios**		
Debt Service Ratio	*0.1*	*0.1 - 0.1*
Financial Obligation Ratio	*0.1*	*0.1 - 0.1*
Consumer Debt Ratio	*0.1*	*0.0 - 0.1*
• **Leverage Ratios**		
Debt Equity Ratio	*0.1*	*0.0 - 0.0*
Debt Income Ratio	*1.8*	*1.5 - 1.6*

Table. 4-26 Ratios summarizing the financial condition of the consumer unit.

Consumer Units Whose Head Is Sixty-five to Seventy-four Years

Consumer units whose head was between sixty-five and seventy-four years consisted of 1.8 people, of which 1.4 were sixty-five years or older. The head was on average 69.1 years. There were only 0.7 wage earners in these consumer units. Their annual income was $47.7 thousand, which is only two-thirds of that in consumer units headed by someone between fifty-five and sixty-four years. Of these consumer units, 81.0 percent owned their homes, of which 37.0 percent had outstanding mortgages.

Consumer units whose head was between sixty-five and seventy-four years had higher disposable income as a percent of gross income than those headed by someone between fifty-five and sixty-four years (94.2 percent versus 89.8 percent). This is, in part, a reflection of their lower gross earnings and income not subject to payroll taxes. Investment income represented 6.4 percent of their gross income in 2007. As a result of having higher fixed, variable, and discretionary obligations than their respective ranges, these consumer units had net income of 10.7 percent of gross income, which is below the target range of 20.1 to 27.9 percent.

	CONSUMER INCOME STATEMENT Head of Consumer Unit Sixty-five to Seventy-four Years	Actual	Range	
	GROSS INCOME	**100.0%**	**100.0%**	**100.0%**
Minus	**PERSONAL TAXES**	**5.8%**	**5.8%**	**- 5.8%**
Minus	**REINVESTMENT INVESTMENT INCOME**	**0.0%**	**0.0%**	**- 0.0%**
Equals	**DISPOSABLE INCOME**	**94.2%**	**94.2%**	**- 94.2%**
Minus	**FIXED OBLIGATIONS**	**33.2%**	**25.4%**	**- 27.4%**
	Housing	15.2%	11.4%	- 12.2%
	Transportation	9.5%	6.0%	- 6.8%
	Health Care	5.9%	5.9%	- 5.9%
	Other	2.5%	2.1%	- 2.5%
Minus	**VARIABLE OBLIGATIONS**	**37.1%**	**31.3%**	**- 35.6%**
	Housing	13.2%	10.3%	- 13.2%
	Food	11.0%	10.2%	- 10.6%
	Transportation	6.2%	4.6%	- 5.4%
	Health Care	3.9%	3.9%	- 3.9%
	Other	2.8%	2.3%	- 2.6%
Minus	**DISCRETIONARY OBLIGATIONS**	**13.3%**	**9.5%**	**- 11.0%**
	Entertainment	31.1%	25.6%	- 29.8%
	Apparel and Services	20.9%	23.5%	- 23.1%
	Tobacco	5.2%	0.0%	- 0.0%
	Other	42.8%	50.9%	- 47.1%
Equals	**NET INCOME**	**10.7%**	**27.9%**	**- 20.1%**

Table. 4-27   Relationship between financial obligations and gross income.

The statement of financial condition of consumer units whose head was between sixty-five and seventy-four years shows current assets of 120.0 percent of gross income, which compares favorably to the desired range of 41.7 to 118.0 percent. However, long-term assets of 2,166.0 percent of gross income are well below the target range of 3,867.2 to 6,131.2 percent. Of particular concern are the nonfinancial assets that comprise 63.3 percent of their long-term assets as compared to a target of 17.9 to 29.3 percent. These long-term assets may need to be liquidated to support these consumer units as they become unable to work and must rely on their assets and social security payments to sustain themselves.

From an obligation perspective, current obligations of 83.5 percent of gross income exceed the target range of 66.2 to 74.0 percent. Long-term obligations of 147.8 percent of gross income also exceed the desired 103.5 to 115.1 percent. As a result, the net worth of these consumer units of 2,054.8 percent of annual gross income is substantially below the 3,839.1 to 6,060.1 percent that constitutes the desired range.

	Actual	Range	
STATEMENT OF FINANCIAL CONDITION			
Head of Consumer Unit Sixty-five to Seventy-four Years			
ASSETS			
CURRENT ASSETS	**120.0%**	**41.7%** -	**118.0%**
Cash	75.2%	40.0% -	17.7%
Short-Term Investments	24.8%	60.0% -	82.3%
LONG-TERM	**2166.0%**	**3967.2%** -	**6131.2%**
Financial Assets	23.3%	7.4% -	4.9%
Retirement Accounts	13.4%	63.2% -	77.2%
Nonfinancial Assets	63.3%	29.3% -	17.9%
TOTAL	**2286.1%**	**4008.8%** -	**6249.3%**
OBLIGATIONS			
CURRENT	**83.5%**	**66.2%** -	**74.0%**
Housing	34.0%	32.8% -	34.2%
Transportation	18.9%	16.0% -	16.4%
Food	13.1%	15.4% -	14.3%
Health Care	11.8%	14.8% -	13.3%
Apparel and Services	3.3%	3.4% -	3.4%
Entertainment	4.9%	3.7% -	4.4%
Other	14.0%	14.0% -	13.9%
LONG-TERM	**147.8%**	**103.5%** -	**115.1%**
Home-Secured Debt	85.8%	96.0% -	92.7%
Installment Loans	6.2%	4.0% -	4.7%
Credit Card Balances	4.4%	0.0% -	1.4%
Other Lines of Credit	1.9%	0.0% -	0.6%
Other Debt	1.7%	0.0% -	0.6%
TOTAL	**231.3%**	**169.7%** -	**189.1%**
NET WORTH	**2054.8%**	**3839.1%** -	**6060.1%**

Table. 4-28   Relationship assets and financial obligations as compared to gross income.

The quaestrological summary for these consumer units shows that their actual income to obligations is below their target ranges. The most significant deficiency in their various ratios is their retirement coverage. It was 2.9 times gross income as compared to a desired range between 25.1 and 47.4 times gross income. This is a situation that could have been avoided had these consumer units more judiciously made spending decisions earlier in their lives.

QUAESTROLOGICAL SUMMARY			
Head of Consumer Unit Sixty-five to Seventy-four Years			
	Actual	Range	
NET WORTH	20.5	38.6 -	60.6
INCOME OBLIGATIONS			
• Fixed Obligations Coverage	3.0	3.7 -	3.9
• Variable Obligations Coverage	2.7	2.8 -	3.2
• Discretionary Obligations Coverage	7.5	9.1 -	10.5
• Income Surplus (Deficit)	0.1	0.2 -	0.3
FINANCIAL CONDITION			
• **Safety Net**	**1.2**	**0.4 -**	**1.2**
• **Long-TermAssets**	**21.7**	**39.7 -**	**61.3**
Financial Assets	*5.1*	*3.0 -*	*3.0*
Nonfinancial Assets	*13.7*	*11.0 -*	*11.6*
Retirement Assets	*2.9*	*25.1 -*	*47.4*
RATIOS			
• **Liquidity Ratios**			
Current Ratio	*17.3*	*7.6 -*	*19.1*
Acid Test	*1.2*	*1.4 -*	*1.5*
• **Indebtedness Ratios**			
Debt Service Ratio	*0.1*	*0.2 -*	*0.2*
Financial Obligation Ratio	*0.2*	*0.1 -*	*0.2*
Consumer Debt Ratio	*0.1*	*0.0 -*	*0.0*
• **Leverage Ratios**			
Debt Equity Ratio	*0.1*	*0.0 -*	*0.0*
Debt Income Ratio	*1.2*	*0.9 -*	*1.0*

Table. 4-29   Ratios summarizing the financial condition of the consumer unit.

Consumer Units Whose Head Is Over Seventy-four Years

In 2007, there were 1.5 persons in consumer units headed by someone over seventy-four years, only 0.2 of which were wage earners. Their income before taxes was $32.5 thousand, which is slightly more than two-thirds of the gross income of consumer units headed by someone between sixty-five and seventy-four years. Over three-quarters of these consumer units were homeowners, of which only 14.3 percent had mortgages. The average age of the heads of these consumer units was 81.5 years. These consumer units rely on their savings, social security, and pensions for their income. Their advanced age and deteriorating health that many of these consumer units must deal with preclude them from working longer.

As was the case with the other consumer units, obligations exceeded the recommended ranges. However, what is different about these consumer units is that their obligations exceeded their income. This means that they had to use their assets to sustain themselves. This should not come as a surprise. This is the very reason that consumer units should start saving for retirement when they are much younger.

CONSUMER INCOME STATEMENT
Head of Consumer Unit Over Seventy-four Years

		Actual	Range	
	GROSS INCOME	**100.0%**	**100.0%**	**100.0%**
Minus	**PERSONAL TAXES**	**3.9%**	**3.9%**	**- 3.9%**
Minus	**REINVESTMENT INVESTMENT INCOME**	**0.0%**	**0.0%**	**- 0.0%**
Equals	**DISPOSABLE INCOME**	**96.1%**	**96.1%**	**- 96.1%**
Minus	**FIXED OBLIGATIONS**	**35.2%**	**18.1%**	**- 23.6%**
	Housing	18.5%	4.6%	- 9.2%
	Transportation	6.5%	4.0%	- 4.6%
	Health Care	8.4%	8.4%	- 8.4%
	Other	1.8%	1.1%	- 1.4%
Minus	**VARIABLE OBLIGATIONS**	**43.7%**	**37.0%**	**- 41.7%**
	Housing	15.9%	11.8%	- 15.2%
	Food	11.5%	10.7%	- 11.1%
	Transportation	6.1%	4.8%	- 5.5%
	Health Care	6.6%	6.6%	- 6.6%
	Other	3.5%	3.1%	- 3.4%
Minus	**DISCRETIONARY OBLIGATIONS**	**21.3%**	**15.6%**	**- 17.9%**
	Entertainment	38.2%	30.5%	- 36.0%
	Apparel and Services	10.6%	11.6%	- 11.6%
	Tobacco	4.8%	0.0%	- 0.0%
	Other	46.4%	57.9%	- 52.4%
Equals	**NET INCOME**	**-3.9%**	**25.4%**	**- 12.9%**

Table. 4-30   Relationship between financial obligations and gross income.

The current assets of consumer units whose head are over seventy-four years represent 184.7 percent of consumer unit annual gross income and are well above the target range of 41.7 to 118.0 percent of gross income. However, long-term assets at 1,832.9 percent of gross income are significantly below the desired range of 3,774.7 to 5,930.9 percent. Furthermore, as with other consumer units, there is a deficiency of retirement assets and an excess of illiquid nonfinancial assets. Current obligations, as well as long-term obligations, are far in excess of the desired ranges. Their respective values of 109.1 percent of gross income and 43.9 percent exceed their respective ranges of 70.7 to 83.2 percent and 27.8 to 31.8 percent.

While percentages have been used in this and previous stratamentical profiles, it may be helpful to use dollars in examining the statement of financial condition for these most senior of consumer units. In terms of dollars, these consumer units were devoting $2.8 thousand of their monthly gross income on current obligations, of which $0.9 thousand was for housing and $0.4 thousand for transportation. Had these consumer units, as may be the case with many, not reduced their current housing and transportation obligations but maintained them at the same rate as they were in consumer units headed by someone between sixty-five and seventy-four, their housing current obligations would have been $1.1 thousand, and their transportation's would have been $0.7 thousand or 63.2 percent of their monthly gross income of $2.8 thousand. Were these consumer units maintaining the same housing and transportation obligations as when their head was between fifty-five and sixty-four years, the drain on their financial assets would have been even worse. Thus the importance of not overextending oneself with fixed obligations.

STATEMENT OF FINANCIAL CONDITION
Head of Consumer Unit Over Seventy-four Years

	Actual	Range	
ASSETS			
CURRENT ASSETS	184.7%	41.7% -	118.0%
Cash	55.0%	40.0% -	17.7%
Short-Term Investments	45.0%	60.0% -	82.3%
LOG TERM	1832.9%	3774.7% -	5930.9%
Financial Assets	29.6%	7.1% -	4.5%
Retirement Accounts	5.3%	66.4% -	79.8%
Nonfinancial Assets	65.0%	26.5% -	15.7%
TOTAL	2017.6%	3816.4% -	6048.9%
OBLIGATIONS			
CURRENT	100.1%	70.7% -	83.2%
Housing	34.4%	23.3% -	29.4%
Transportation	12.6%	12.5% -	12.2%
Food	11.5%	15.1% -	13.3%
Health Care	15.0%	21.2% -	18.0%
Apparel and Services	2.3%	2.6% -	2.5%
Entertainment	8.1%	6.7% -	7.7%
Other	16.3%	18.6% -	16.9%
LONG-TERM	43.9%	27.8% -	31.8%
Home-Secured Debt	78.7%	95.5% -	89.7%
Installment Loans	5.1%	4.5% -	4.7%
Credit Card Balances	5.1%	0.0% -	1.8%
Other Lines of Credit	2.9%	0.0% -	1.0%
Other Debt	8.2%	0.0% -	2.8%
TOTAL	144.0%	98.6% -	114.9%
NET WORTH	1873.6%	3717.8% -	5934.0%

Table. 4-31   Relationship assets and financial obligations as compared to gross income.

What had been said about consumer units headed by someone between sixty-five and seventy-four is even truer for these consumer units. Incomes are unable to safely satisfy obligations, assets are too concentrated in nonfnancial assets, and there are inadequate retirement assets. Whether these consumer units are able to maintain their financial independence is a function of how long their memebrs will live and the state of their health.

QUAESTROLOGICAL SUMMARY Head of Consumer Unit Over Seventy-four Years			
	Actual	**Range**	
NET WORTH	18.7	37.2 -	59.3
INCOME OBLIGATIONS			
• Fixed Obligations Coverage	2.9	4.3 -	5.7
• Variable Obligations Coverage	2.2	2.2 -	2.6
• Discretionary Obligations Coverage	4.7	5.6 -	6.4
• Income Surplus (Deficit)	(0.1)	0.1 -	0.2
FINANCIAL CONDITION			
• **Safety Net**	**1.8**	**0.4 -**	**1.2**
• **Long-TermAssets**	**18.3**	**37.7 -**	**59.3**
Financial Assets	5.4	2.7 -	2.7
Nonfinancial Assets	11.9	9.3 -	10.0
Retirement Assets	1.0	25.1 -	47.4
RATIOS			
• **Liquidity Ratios**			
Current Ratio	4.8	7.1 -	7.1
Acid Test	1.0	1.2 -	1.4
• **Indebtedness Ratios**			
Debt Service Ratio	0.0	0.1 -	0.1
Financial Obligation Ratio	0.1	0.1 -	0.1
Consumer Debt Ratio	0.1	0.0 -	0.2
• **Leverage Ratios**			
Debt Equity Ratio	0.	0.0 -	0.0
Debt Income Ratio	0.2	0.2 -	0.2

Table. 4-32   Ratios summarizing the financial condition of the consumer unit.

PRESCRIPTIONS

When our physiology indicates a problem with our health, there are a range of treatment options that our physician may choose from. They range from let's watch the condition and see if it corrects itself, let's do further tests, stop smoking or indulging in other deleterious habits, take this medicine and see if the condition improves, or to more radical options such as surgery. Unfortunately, when it comes to our quaestrology, there is only one basic prescription, and that it is to change our lifestyle. This involves curbing unnecessary expenditures and investing our savings. It also means limiting our use of credit and other forms of debt to finance our current way of living. Debt may be acceptable when used to finance long-term assets. However, it is not okay to use it as a means of financing current consumption on everyday needs such as food and discretionary items such as apparel and entertainment. With this simple concept in mind, the following prescriptions have been written to assist the consumer unit in getting its finances in order.

Financial Security

<table>
<tr><td colspan="11" align="center">Personal Wealth Maker
Gold Paved Street
Wealthville, USA</td></tr>
<tr><td colspan="11" align="center">**Age of Consumer Unit Head**</td></tr>
<tr><td>All</td><td>X</td><td><35</td><td>☐</td><td>35–44 ☐</td><td>45–54 ☐</td><td>55–64 ☐</td><td>65–74 ☐</td><td>>74 ☐</td></tr>
</table>

- *Define financial security.*

☐ _____

Depending on the age of the consumer unit, financial security has different meanings. In the youngest consumer units, there are the needs to establish a home, embark on a career path, start a family, etc. As the age of the consumer unit increases, so do its needs. Middle-age units become more concerned with educating their children and preparing for retirement. Whereas the oldest units are most concerned with not outliving their money. Irrespective of the age of the consumer unit, the basic steps are as follows:

- Define financial security. There is no universal definition of financial security. For some, it may mean being able to buy whatever they want whenever they want it. For others, it may mean having enough investment income to support themselves, being able to buy that first car or house, paying for the education of their children, being able to travel extensively during retirement or being unencumbered by debt of any sort. Unless financial security is defined, it is almost impossible to know if it has been achieved.

- Identify measures of success. Success should be quantified so that it can be measured. Typical examples of these measures include a specific annual income, retirement assets, safety net, net worth, value of investments, debt levels, etc.
- Define assumptions. Every plan is based on a certain set of assumptions, and the plan for achieving financial security is no different. Assumptions might include factors such as the number of earners in the consumer unit, whether to rent or own a home, number of children to have, amount of income that is to be saved, estimated rates of return on investments, retirement age, etc.
- Prepare time line. For each of the measures of success, a time frame for achieving each one should be prepared. These time lines should be segmented into five-year increments with specific objectives to be achieved at the end of each time period.

For example, let us assume that a consumer unit headed by someone under thirty-five years has defined financial security as having an investment income of $25,000 a year by the time its head retires. The time line might show having annual investment income of $2,500 by the age of forty, $5,000 by forty-five, $7,500 by fifty, $10,000 by fifty-five, $15,000 by sixty, and $20,000 by the age of sixty-five. Unless there were these interim milestones, the consumer unit might delude itself into thinking that it was on track to achieve its goal only to discover that it was way off track and had no reasonable expectation of achieving its financial security.

Income-Expenditure Relationships

Personal Wealth Maker
Gold Paved Street
Wealthville, USA

Age of Consumer Unit Head

All [X]   <35 [ ]   35–44 [ ]   45–54 [ ]   55–64 [ ]   65–74 [ ]   >74 [ ]

- *Determine relationships between consumer unit income and expenditures.*

[ ] _____

The importance of living within one's means cannot be overemphasized. It is only when there is something left over after satisfying one's financial obligations can one have any reasonable expectation of achieving his/her financial security. In managing the relationship between consumer unit income and expenditures, it is necessary to do the following:

- **Estimate income**. The first step in estimating income is to determine the number of earners there will be in the consumer unit and what each one can reasonably expected to earn. Income should be based on regular income and not include overtime pay, bonuses, or any other form of incentive compensation. Ideally, investment income from interest, dividends, capital gains, rent, etc., should not be considered as income unless one or more of the consumer unit's members is retired, disabled, or not working.
- **Define lifestyle**. It is important for the consumer unit to determine what its priorities are as this will determine its cost of living. If the consumer unit wants to enjoy lavish vacations,

expensive cars, luxurious homes, etc., then it may be extremely difficult, if not impossible, for younger consumer units to achieve this lifestyle. However, older consumer units that have created substantial income-producing assets may indeed be able to indulge themselves.

- **Determine expenditures**. Based on the lifestyle that the consumer unit has chosen, it should identify the associated costs. Costs should be segmented into housing, transportation, food, health care, apparel and services, entertainment, and other. Each of these cost categories should be divided into their fixed and variable components.

- **Prepare budget**. Using the consumer income statement as a guide, enter estimated income and expenditures. If there is insufficient income to satisfy all of the consumer unit's financial obligations, then the consumer unit must decide whether to redefine its lifestyle so that it can live within its means or to assume debt in order to achieve its desired lifestyle. It is important to remember that unless the consumer unit has achieved its definition of financial security, having enough income to cover financial obligations is not enough. There must also be residual income that can be invested in its future.

- **Monitor progress.** Having a budget in itself is insufficient to properly manage the relationship between income and expenditures. One must determine the validity of the budget. To do so, actual income and expenditures should be compared against budgeted amounts. Fortunately, there is software available to assist in the necessary bookkeeping. If expenditures are not within budgeted parameters, then it may be necessary to reduce expenditures or seek out additional sources of income. In the short run, the only expenditures that can be reduced are those that are either discretionary or variable. If there is a significant difference between income and expenditures, then it might be necessary to redefine the consumer unit's lifestyle expectations.

Safety Net

Personal Wealth Maker
Gold Paved Street
Wealthville, USA

Age of Consumer Unit Head

All	[X]	<35 [ ]	35–44 [ ]	45–54 [ ]	55–64 [ ]	65–74 [ ]	>74 [ ]

℞

- *Establish a safety net for unforeseen financial needs.*

□ _____

While there are numerous prescriptions for preparing for foreseeable financial needs, perhaps the most important one is to establish a safety net that can be used if the consumer unit has financial obligations that cannot be satisfied with current income. A safety net is a pool of liquid assets whose sole purpose is to be available in case of a minor financial problem or a more severe one. The safety net asset pool is measured in month's income. Sometimes it is an unexpected bill such as a large repair or medical bill. In other cases, it may be of much more dire consequences such as the loss of job or disability, situations in which there may be a loss of income for weeks or even months. As the age of the head of the consumer unit increases, the probability of one or more income earners becoming disabled or unemployed increases. Therefore, the size of the safety net, i.e., the number of months' income should increase as the consumer unit ages. A useful guide in determining minimum safety nets is as follows:

Age of Consumer Unit Head	Safety Net	Age of Consumer Unit Head	Safety Net
<35	4 months' income	55–64	12 months' income
35–44	6 months' income	65–74	18 months' income
45–54	8 months' income	>74	18 months' income

Consumer units whose head is retired face the prospect of large medical bills that might not be fully covered by insurance. In such cases, it is important that the safety net be sufficient to supplement insurance coverage.

Education of Children

Personal Wealth Maker
Gold Paved Street
Wealthville, USA

Age of Consumer Unit Head

| All ☐ | <35 ☐ | X 35–44 | X 45–54 | 55–64 ☐ | 65–74 ☐ | >74 ☐ |

- *Prepare plan for financing education of children.*

The proper education of one's children is one of the most important challenges facing the consumer unit. Certain consumer units may feel quite comfortable with the quality of public education where they live. Others may feel it necessary to send their children to private or boarding schools. Since parents should encourage their children to attend college, the consumer unit should start saving for college as soon as possible. Depending on scholarships or education loans to finance a child's college education is not the responsible thing to do. Obviously, the more children in the family, the more money will be needed. In ensuring that funds will be needed to support the education of their children, consumer units should:

- Define K-12 education needs. If the consumer unit decides that its children will attend public schools, then there are no financial obligations that need to be accounted for. If, on the other hand, it determines that private education is appropriate for one or more of its children, then it must decide at which grade level it will send them to a private school. Admission standards for private school should be determined and steps taken to ensure that the prospective student(s) can satisfy the requirements.
- Define college requirements. It is never too early to start saving for college. If one is fortunate to live in an area such as Boston where there is an abundance of colleges and universities, then commuting to college from home may be an option. However, if one lives in a rural area, then commuting is probably not an option. Whether, the child will be able to satisfy the admission requirements of an Ivy League school is certainly something that the proud parent cannot know until the child has taken the college admission tests. However, the prudent assumption to make is that the child will be able to gain admission to the college or university of his/her choosing.
- Determine costs. Based on the assumptions that have been made concerning the education of the children in the consumer unit, estimates must be made as to the associated costs. These costs include, obviously, tuition and books as well as room and board or commuting costs as well as incidentals. If the child is to attend school away from home, then costs of traveling to and from school during vacation periods should also be included. In determining these costs, one should take the current costs and adjust for their anticipated annual increases. If college tuition costs are increasing at 5 percent a year, then the cost of sending a five-year-old to college at the age of eighteen could be more than twice the current costs.
- Develop savings investment strategy. Investing to educate children is no different than any other investment strategy. There are variables that are completely within your control, and those that are beyond your control. The only variables that you can control are the amount of money to be invested and

the duration of the investment. Historical rates of return can be helpful in selecting investments. However, actual rates may, and probably will, differ considerably from what were historical norms. Reducing the amount of money that is invested and/ or shortening the duration of the investment means that there needs to be a higher return in order to meet your objectives. This is also true if actual returns are less than the historical norms upon which an investment strategy was formulated.

- Monitor progress. One does not want to wait until his/her Rhodes scholar to be is ready to attend college to learn that there are insufficient funds to pay for tuition and the associated costs of a college education. Therefore, the performance of the college education fund must be monitored on a regular basis, no more frequently than quarterly and more frequently than annually. If actual performance is less than anticipated, then consider increasing contributions to the education fund or reallocating funds to other assets classes. However, one should not expose the portfolio to undue risk. As the date that junior will attend college approaches, safety of principal becomes a more important consideration than capital appreciation.

Retirement Planning

Personal Wealth Maker
Gold Paved Street
Wealthville, USA

			Age of Consumer Unit Head				
All	[X] <35	[ ] 35–44	[ ] 45–54	[ ] 55–64	[ ] 65–74	[ ] >74	

• *Prepare a retirement plan.*

When we are starting out in our careers, thinking about a life in retirement that is thirty or more years away is something that many put off until the proverbial tomorrow. It is often the case that many find themselves approaching retirement without adequate financial resources to sustain then during retirement. The uncertain nature of future Social Security benefits places the onus on the individual to ensure that retirement will not be a nightmare. While there are many financial challenges facing young consumer units, retirement planning is one that should not be postponed. Effective retirement planning consists of the following:

- **Taking advantage of employer-sponsored retirement plans**. Few employers offer defined-benefit retirement programs. Instead, they offer defined-contribution plans. Those employees who are fortunate enough to have an employer who offers retirement savings plans should take advantage of these programs as soon as they are eligible to participate. Remember that the sooner you start saving for retirement, the less you will need to contribute, and the lower the return on your investment will be needed to meet your objective. Employee contributions come from pretax dollars, which is an advantage that should not be overlooked. Often the employer will match a portion of the employee's contribution. This is a gift that should be taken advantage of.

- **Determining asset allocation**. Typically, retirement plans offer choices as to where the contributions are invested. As with all investments, the importance of diversification cannot be overemphasized. It is best that these funds be invested in a broadly based index or mutual fund. No matter how promising an employer's prospects may be, it would behoove the employee to not over concentrate his/her retirement assets in the employer's stock. One cannot afford its stock tanking just as one is approaching retirement as was the case with Enron.
- **Defining retirement goals**. When the head of the consumer unit is between forty-five and fifty-four years, many of the obligations associated with raising a family have been taken care of. This is the ideal time for the consumer unit to discuss its retirement goals. Things that should be considered are the age at which the unit's earners will retire, where to live during retirement, amount of traveling, hobbies to pursue, etc.
- **Monitoring progress**. As with all investment programs, the performance of the retirement portfolio must be regularly monitored. As the consumer unit's retirement goals are clarified, the adequacy of the portfolio must be evaluated. If the portfolio appears to not be on track to meet the unit's retirement goals, then either the goals must be less ambitious, the earners need to work longer, or more money must be allocated to retirement assets.

Investment Planning

Personal Wealth Maker
Gold Paved Street
Wealthville, USA

Age of Consumer Unit Head

All [X] <35 [ ] 35–44 [ ] 45–54 [ ] 55–64 [ ] 65–74 [ ] >74 [ ]

• *Analyze the implications of any potential investment.*

[ ] _____

Too often when making an investment, an inordinate amount of effort is devoted to estimating potential returns and neglecting the implications of the investment and the potential risks. Many investors have unrealistic expectations for the returns they anticipate. The average annual return from 1928–2008 of an investment in large capitalization growth stocks was 11.1 percent; in large capitalization value stocks, 15.1 percent; in small capitalization growth stocks, 11.1 percent; in small capitalization value stocks, 18.5 percent; and in S&P 500 index, 12.0 percent. During that same time period, annual inflation averaged 3.2 percent. From 1958 to 2008, the yields on six month T-Bills averaged 5.6 percent; from 1964 to 2008, certificates of deposit averaged 4.5 percent; from 1962 to 2008, five-year treasury notes averaged 2.5 percent and ten treasury bonds averaged 7.0 percent. While recent returns have differed from these averages, it is still instructive to compare them against historical averages in projected anticipated returns on future investments.

Perhaps one of the more important concerns of investors is the safety of principal. The shorter the investment time horizon, the more defensive the investment should be. This means that money should be placed in certificates of deposit, FDIC insured savings accounts, and treasuries. As the investment time horizon becomes longer, then riskier investment classes such as equities become more appropriate. Irrespective of the investment opportunity, investors should satisfy themselves that the risk of losing their principal is manageable.

Inflation, the erosion in the purchasing power of the dollar, must be considered in planning one's investments. While inflation has not been an issue for investors in recent years, it should not be taken lightly. From 1914 to 2008, inflation averaged 3.45 percent per year. This means that it would take $25.08 in 2008 dollars to purchase what $1.00 would have bought in 1914. From 1928 to 2008, inflation out performed equity and fixed income investments 9.9 percent of the time.

Returns from an investment come from two sources, income and capital appreciation. Those who need funds to sustain their current lifestyle need current income. For these investors, it is important to consider not only the rate of return, but also the certainty that such payments will, in fact, be received. Others, whose investment needs are longer term, tend to prefer capital appreciation. This is not to say that an investment can't produce both current income and long-term appreciation. Dividend paying stocks and rental property are examples of investments that generate current returns in the form of dividends and rent as well as long-term capital appreciation potential.

Being fortunate enough to have invested in a financially lucrative opportunity is great. However, one should also be concerned about the liquidity of the investment. For certain investment classes, such as stocks and bonds, there are liquid markets in which they can be sold, and the value received in a matter of days. Other investments, such as real estate, can take months to monetize. Investments in partnerships can take even longer to liquidate and often at substantial discounts to the underlying value. The lesson here is to be sure that all investments can be liquidated within your investment time horizon.

Credit Cards

Personal Wealth Maker
Gold Paved Street
Wealthville, USA

Age of Consumer Unit Head

| All | X | <35 | ☐ | 35–44 | ☐ | 45–54 | ☐ | 55–64 | ☐ | 65–74 | ☐ | >74 | ☐ |

- *Use credit cards wisely.*

A credit card issued by a bank or other financial company allows the holder an option to defer payment on purchases. They charge interest on balances not paid in full at the end of the billing period. They should be used as a convenience not as a means of purchasing things that are not affordable. Not having to carry large sums of cash or having to write checks every time something is purchased is the proper use of a credit card. It is not a means of deferring payment for months or even years. This means that consumer units should not carry balances from billing cycle to billing cycle. The financial burden of such practices will last far longer than the momentary euphoria of the initial purchase. Consumer units should utilize credit cards that do not charge annual fees.

Credit card companies and certain merchants offer incentives to use their cards. Certain of these offers are good and should be taken advantage of. With regard to the others, beware of credit card companies bearing gifts. Credit card company offers of extra rebates of extra cash back bonuses on certain kinds of purchases and of extra discounts from selected merchants represent opportunities that make sense if the consumer unit was going to purchase the item anyway. For example, a $10 discount when you spend $50 on office supplies is a good deal if you need the items. If you have no use for such items, then this represents a purchase best not made. Another example is the no money down, no interest, and no payments for twelve months' offer. This is a good deal if you have the discipline and money to pay off the entire balance before the end of the offer. If not, this could be an expensive deal.

Long-Term Obligations

Personal Wealth Maker
Gold Paved Street
Wealthville, USA

Age of Consumer Unit Head

All		<35		35–44	X	45–54	X	55–64	X	65–74	X	>74	

℞

• *Ensure that income will be available to meet fixed and variable costs over life of obligation.*

There reaches a time for most consumer units when there is a reduction in income. This usually occurs as the earners in the consumer unit approach retirement age. While every consumer unit is different, most will experience a reduction in income when the consumer unit's head is between forty-five and fifty-four years. Even if income does not decline, the chances of a loss of income due to disability or loss of job increase in such consumer units. While finding a new job at comparable pay may be difficult for these consumer units, the task becomes even more daunting for older ones. Therefore, assuming large long-term obligations in older consumer units is something that should be done only after careful analysis of the implications on the financial stability of the consumer unit. A thirty-year mortgage that requires a $2,500 per month payment may be affordable for a consumer unit that is earning $10,000 a month. However, if the consumer unit's income becomes $4,000 a month during retirement what once was affordable becomes unaffordable. Under such circumstances, the consumer unit would be faced with difficult choices such as drastically decreasing all other expenditures or selling the house. While younger consumer units should also be wary of overextending themselves financially, they also will most probably see their income increase and thus make such obligations more affordable in the future.

Variable Interest Rate Mortgages

Personal Wealth Maker
Gold Paved Street
Wealthville, USA

Age of Consumer Unit Head

All		<35	35–44	45–54	55–64	65–74	>74
	X	☐	☐	☐	☐	☐	☐

℞

• *Beware of variable interest mortgages.*

☐ _____

A mortgage is a loan that is secured by a specific piece of real estate in which the borrower repays the original balance as well as interest accrued over the course of the loan. Variable interest rate or floating rate mortgages basically are mortgages whose rate of interest may change over the course of the mortgage. These rates fluctuate in accordance with the rate upon which they are based. LIBOR (London Interbank Offered Rate) and COFI (11th District Cost of Funds Index) are two of the more popular benchmarks that are used in setting the interest rate on these loans. Sometimes these mortgages offer an initial fixed rate or teaser rate that is fixed for a number of months and then fluctuates in accordance with their benchmark.

Since the monthly payments for these floating rate mortgages can change and sometimes significantly over their lifetime, they should be taken out with caution. If mortgage rates are at or near historic lows, then taking out such mortgages exposes the mortgagee to potentially higher monthly payments that he/she may not be able to afford should prevailing interest rates increase to or above their long-term average rate. When interest rates are at historic highs, then such mortgages may be advisable especially if the rates are fixed for five or more years. Assuming a mortgage that only with cheater rates is affordable and betting that the underlying value of the property will increase so that it can be sold at a profit before the mortgage rate resets to a higher rate is a bet that the recent decline in house values has shown to be ill-advised.

As a general rule, variable rate mortgages should be avoided. If the consumer unit cannot afford the house of its dreams, it should redefine its dream house so that it is affordable or defer purchasing it until such time as the consumer unit can afford it.

Mortgage Refinancing

Personal Wealth Maker
Gold Paved Street
Wealthville, USA

Age of Consumer Unit Head

| All | X | <35 | ☐ | 35–44 | ☐ | 45–54 | ☐ | 55–64 | ☐ | 65–74 | ☐ | >74 | ☐ |

• *Before refinancing, do the math.*

Many homeowners from time to time will consider refinancing the outstanding mortgage on their property. There are two basic reasons for homeowners to consider such action. The first is to take equity out of their home. This action will increase the outstanding loan balance, which will typically be paid out over thirty years. A better way to accomplish this goal is the use of an equity line of credit, which typically has lower interest rates. It should be noted that since equity lines of credit typically have variable interest rates, they could, over the course of the loan, end up with a higher interest rate than a fixed-rate mortgage. However, unless the home equity can earn a higher a rate of return than the loan rate or cost less than, say, a car loan, it would be best not to take equity out of the home.

The second reason to refinance a home mortgage is to take advantage of a lower interest rate. However, it may not always be beneficial to take advantage of lower interest rates. Rather than concentrating on the reduced monthly payment, one should examine the total outlay over the course of the existing loan and the new one. The number of years remaining on the existing loan is crucial in determining the advisability of refinancing. As the following chart illustrates, the allocation of monthly mortgage payments that go to interest and principal changes with the time the loan has remaining. In the early years of the loan, the majority of the payment goes toward interest, not toward reducing principal. As the mortgage approached maturity, the majority of the payments go toward paying down principal. In the early years of the mortgage, it may be appropriate to refinance the mortgage. This would depend on the transaction costs involved as well as the differential in interest rates. The analysis involves comparing the outstanding payments on the existing mortgage to the payments over the life of the new mortgage plus the associated transaction costs as appraisals, points, and other fees. Depending on the number of years remaining on the original mortgage it, taking out a new mortgage with a shorter length might make sense, i.e., replacing a thirty-year mortgage with a fifteen-year one. The option with the lower total cost is the one to choose. If the consumer unit cannot consistently cover its current mortgage payments, then refinancing may be appropriate irrespective of the results of the preceding analysis.

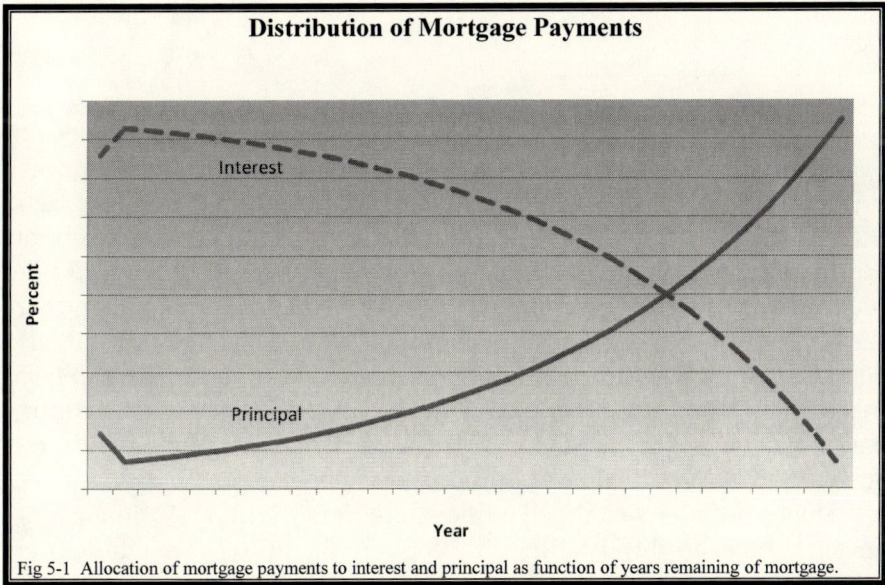

Distribution of Mortgage Payments

Interest

Percent

Principal

Year

Fig 5-1 Allocation of mortgage payments to interest and principal as function of years remaining of mortgage.

Lines of Credit

Personal Wealth Maker
Gold Paved Street
Wealthville, USA

Age of Consumer Unit Head

All	X	<35	☐	35–44	☐	45–54	☐	55–64	☐	65–74	☐	>74	☐

℞

• *Utilize lines of credit judiciously.*

☐ _____

Lines of credit can be an important component of a consumer unit's financial strategy. Just as with credit cards and other forms of debt, there are wise uses of it as well as foolish uses. It can be used for home improvements. It can also be used in lieu of car loans and the ilk. Other uses include paying for college and other expenditures that improve the consumer unit's ability to generate income. Lines of credit can also be looked at as an additional safety net. It should not be used as an ATM machine to finance recurring current financial obligations on a routine basis. Nor should it be used to splurge on ego-satisfying expenditures such as jewels, extravagant vacations, etc.

The best time to establish a line of credit is when one's finances are strong. It is exceedingly difficult to obtain a loan in cases where there are outstanding credit card balances, late mortgage payments, and especially when one is unemployed. When one needs a line of credit the most is when it is the most difficult to obtain one.

Vehicle Purchases

Personal Wealth Maker
Gold Paved Street
Wealthville, USA

Age of Consumer Unit Head

All		<35	35–44	45–54	55–64	65–74	>74
	X	☐	☐	☐	☐	☐	☐

℞

- *Carefully analyze purchase options.*

After a house, the automobile is the second largest purchase most consumer units will make. With automobiles costing $30 thousand or significantly more, consumer units should carefully consider their options before making such a purchase. The first and foremost question to be answered is, why is the car being purchased? If it is to replace a vehicle that has outlived its useful life, then such a purchase would seem to make good economic sense. If it is to reinforce one's ego, then such a purchase is not a wise decision. Keeping a vehicle that is in good condition an extra year or two or more can do wonders in improving the quaestrology of the consumer unit.

Assuming that the consumer unit really needs to acquire another vehicle, then the issues become new vs. used, trade-in vs. sales by owner, and purchase vs. lease. The decision to purchase a new or used vehicle from an economic perspective would favor buying cars that are two to three years old. Since an automobile loses 25 percent of its value, a three-year-old car can be purchased for around 45 percent of a new one. If the car has low mileage and has been well maintained, then such a purchase can make sense. Older cars may have higher mileage and may not have been well maintained and, therefore, should be bought with extreme caution. In cases where the new car is replacing another within the consumer unit, it is best to try and sell it yourself. By doing so, it is possible to receive more than a dealer would have allowed if the vehicle had been traded in. If the consumer unit needs, as opposed to wants, a new car every five years, it probably makes economic sense to lease the vehicle assuming that the lease's mileage allowance is adequate. In all other cases, the car should be purchased. Whether leasing or purchasing the new car, prospective buyers should ascertain what such vehicles are actually selling for as opposed to the sticker price. While all those fancy accessories may be nice, everyone should determine whether they are really needed.

Ideally, a consumer unit should pay cash for its automobile purchases. However, for most, this will not be the case. Low interest financing options are often offered by car dealers. Sometimes they even offer zero percent financing. In any case where the dealer is offering zero percent financing, it is a financial gift that should not be turned down. In other cases, the dealer may still be offering the best rate. However, it would be wise to check out other financing options such as those offered by banks or credit unions. Those consumer units that have an equity line of credit should consider using that as a source of funds to purchase the new vehicle. This would make sense if the interest rate on the line of credit was lower than other financing options. Another advantage is that under current IRS regulations interest payments on lines of credit are tax deductible. Since interest rates on home equity lines of credit are typically variable, the borrower faces the risk of potentially paying higher interest rates over the course of the loan. Car loans typically have fixed interest rates.

Nonfinancial Assets

Personal Wealth Maker
Gold Paved Street
Wealthville, USA

		Age of Consumer Unit Head					
All [X]	<35 [ ]	35–44 [ ]	45–54 [ ]	55–64 [ ]	65–74 [ ]	>74 [ ]	

℞

- *Don't concentrate wealth in nonfinancial assets.*

Nonfinancial assets consist of items with a physical value. Examples of nonfinancial assets include jewelry, land, houses, vehicles, etc. Unlike financial assets, the value of nonfinancial assets is not set by financial markets such as the New York Stock Exchange but by estimates of what the item might bring if sold. These estimates are typically based on the sales prices of comparable items. Unlike financial assets, it can take weeks or months to consummate a sale of nonfinancial assets. Furthermore, certain nonfinancial assets lose value every year.

Having a disproportionate allocation of one's wealth in nonfinancial assets can lead to a false sense of financial security. Monetizing nonfinancial assets can be a time-consuming process that can generate less money than the estimated value in the statement of financial condition. Unfortunately, the net worth of most consumer units is concentrated in their home, which obviously is not a financial asset. Furthermore, currently it is estimated that approximately 10 percent of homeowners have negative equity, i.e., the outstanding mortgages and other hoe debt exceed the value of the property.

Insurance

Personal Wealth Maker
Gold Paved Street
Wealthville, USA

Age of Consumer Unit Head

| All | X | <35 | ☐ | 35–44 | ☐ | 45–54 | ☐ | 55–64 | ☐ | 65–74 | ☐ | >74 | ☐ |

- *Be sure that the consumer unit is adequately protected.*

The consumer unit needs for insurance protection changes as the consumer unit ages. All consumer units need health, home, life, and car insurance. The coverage of these insurance policies should be tailored to the individual needs of the consumer unit. Since younger consumer units have less net worth than older ones, it is important that the unit's breadwinners have adequate life insurance in the unlikely event of the death of one of them. Older consumer units should consider long-term care policies that are consistent with the type of coverage they need. Irrespective of the age of the consumer unit, long-term disability policies should also be considered so that, in the words of the famous duck, *"it won't hurt to miss work."* Consumer units should determine the need for additional coverage, such as higher limits on liability coverage, than in the standard homeowner policy, earthquake policies, and flood insurance. The proper amount of insurance protection is something that each consumer unit must determine for itself.

Quaestrology Management

Personal Wealth Maker
Gold Paved Street
Wealthville, USA

Age of Consumer Unit Head

All	<35	35–44	45–54	55–64	65–74	>74
[X]	☐	☐	☐	☐	☐	☐

- *Monitor consumer unit's quaestrology.*

☐ _____

Quaestrology provides a benchmark against which each consumer unit, irrespective of the age of its head, can evaluate its financial health. It tracks the flow of the unit's income, the assets that it has accumulated, the financial obligations that it has incurred, and its resulting net worth. It is critical for the consumer unit to understand its quaestrology, i.e., where it stands financially. It should prepare a consumer income statement, statement of financial condition, and quaestrological summary. Ideally, this should be done on a quarterly basis but no less frequently than annually. The actual values of the elements in each statement should be compared against the consumer unit's target range. In addition, the progress against each milestone should be evaluated and adjustments made as appropriate. If progress is not acceptable, then the consumer unit should consider seeking ways to increase its income, reduce its financial obligations, and/or change its priorities.

CONCLUDING THOUGHTS

Many otherwise intelligent people feel that finances are too complicated to understand and, therefore, choose to not think about their financial situation. If they are able to pay the bill they receive today, then they deem themselves to be financially solvent. Such an approach can, in most cases, lead to an unfortunate outcome. If the reader has gained nothing else from reading this book, he/she should at least start the process of considering the long-term implications of the financial decisions that he/she makes. Discretionary financial obligations should be viewed as expenditures that can most easily be reduced. Not incurring a particular expense, while it certainly will not provide gratification, will allow one to sleep better knowing that there is one less bill or series of bills to be paid. Variable obligations too can be more tightly managed if one so chooses. Of all the financial obligations that a consumer unit (family) incurs, fixed obligations can be the most detrimental to its quaestrology. These obligations often must be satisfied over five years in the case of an automobile purchase that was financed to as long as thirty years in the case of the typical home mortgage. Assuming such burdens that might not be sustainable if income does not increase as much as hoped for or if income actually decreases over the life of the obligation is not the financially prudent thing to do. Planning on continually earning oversized commissions or bonuses to cover luxuries is understandable for discretionary items but dangerous for purchases that are financed over many years.

While preparing budgets and monitoring expenditures can be a daunting task, it should not deter one from starting to take control of his/her finances. One should establish a process whereby portions of one's income are regularly set aside to cover anticipated future needs such as buying a home, educating one's children, etc. Certainly, taking advantage of employer-subsidized retirement plans is something that should be taken advantage of at the earliest opportunity. Any bonuses or financial windfalls should be viewed as an opportunity to put some money away for future needs. Similarly, increases in salary should also represent opportunities to increase savings. There is minimal sacrifice in saving a portion of something that one was able to survive without in the past. While amassing wealth can appear to be a daunting task, delaying the process only makes it the more daunting.

Throughout this book, the importance of not incurring obligations that cannot be satisfied with one's income has been repeatedly stressed. In particular, the importance of not incurring obligations during preretirement years that cannot be met with retirement income is a situation that one does not want to find himself/herself. The following chart plots the previously described relationships of available income and financial obligations as a function of the age of the head of the consumer unit. In 2007, available income continued to increase percent until the age of the head of the consumer unit was between forty-five and fifty-four years. The available income of these consumer units was 138.7 percent of the younger ones. There was a continuing decline in financial obligations as represented by the solid financial obligations-A line, which depicts consumer units whose head is between thirty-five and forty-four years of 123.2 percent of the youngest consumer units. From that high point, it steadily declines to 74.8 percent in the oldest consumer units. Under this condition, the available income of this segment of consumer units is 60.4 percent of the youngest. If, as depicted in financial obligations-B line, consumer units whose head is of retirement age were to maintain the same level of financial obligations that they had when that head was between fifty-five and sixty-four years, then their financial obligations would remain at 114.2 percent of consumer units headed by someone under thirty-five years. To support those obligations, consumer units whose head was between sixty-five and seventy-four years had 86.9 percent of consumer units headed by someone under thirty-five years; units whose head was older than seventy-four years had 60.4 percent.

Available Income versus Financial Obligations
(<35 = 100)

Available Income

Financial Obligations-B

Financial Obligations-A

Age of Head of Consumer Unit

| Fig. 6-1 | Relationships between consumer unit available income and financial obligations as a function of the age of head of consumer unit. |
| Data: | *2007 Federal Reserve Survey Consumer Finances* |

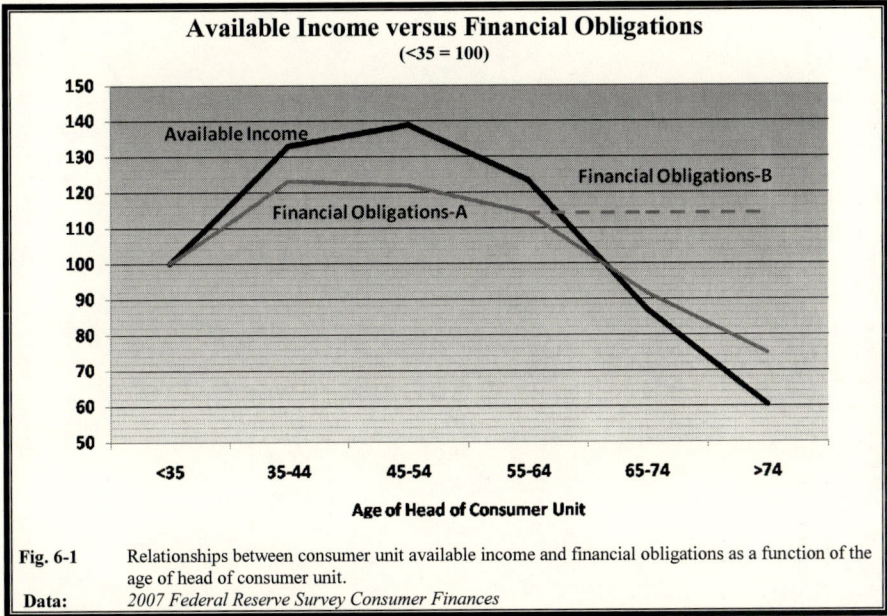

From a practical perspective, it may be difficult to adjust one's financial obligations as one's sources of income decrease in retirement. If one has financial assets set aside for retirement, then one can withdraw those funds to meet his/her financial obligations. If this is not the case, then there are two options. The first is to continue to work during retirement years to generate additional income. The second is to reduce one's standard of living. With proper planning, retirement years can be golden years.

APPENDICES

Consumer Income Statements

Head Under Thirty-five years

CONSUMER INCOME STATEMENT TARGET RANGES Head Under Thirty-five Years					
GROSS INCOME			**100.0%**	**-**	**100.0%**
Wages and salaries	92.4%	- 92.4%			
Self-employment income	4.4%	- 4.4%			
Social Security, private and government retirement	0.5%	- 0.5%			
Interest, dividends, rental income, other property income	0.7%	- 0.7%			
Unemployment and workers' compensation, veterans' benefits	0.3%	- 0.3%			
Public assistance, supplemental security income, food stamps	0.6%	- 0.6%			
Regular contributions for support	0.7%	- 0.7%			
Other income	0.5%	- 0.5%			
PERSONAL TAXES			**9.7%**	**-**	**9.7%**
Federal income taxes	1.7%	- 1.7%			
State and local income taxes	0.7%	- 0.7%			
FICA	7.1%	- 7.1%			
Other taxes	0.2%	- 0.2%			
Investment income reinvestment			-0.7%	-	0.0%
DISPOSABLE INCOME			**89.7%**	**-**	**90.3%**
FIXED OBLIGATIONS			**29.2%**	**-**	**31.8%**
Housing			17.5%	-	18.4%
• Shelter	17.5%	- 18.4%			
Transportation			8.2%	-	9.8%
• Vehicles purchases	5.7%	- 6.9%			
• Vehicle finance charges	0.6%	- 0.7%			
• Vehicle insurance	1.2%	- 1.4%			
• Other vehicle expenses	0.7%	- 0.9%			
Health care			1.6%	-	1.6%
• Health insurance	1.6%	- 1.6%			
Other			1.9%	-	1.9%
• Life and other personal insurance	0.3%	- 0.3%			
• Pensions	1.7%	- 1.7%			
VARIABLE OBLIGATIONS			**28.8%**	**-**	**32.2%**
Housing			10.2%	-	11.9%
• Utilities, fuels, and public services	4.5%	- 5.3%			
• Household operations	1.8%	- 2.1%			
• Housekeeping supplies	0.8%	- 0.9%			
• Household furnishings and equipment	3.0%	- 3.6%			

CONSUMER INCOME STATEMENT TARGET RANGES
Head Under Thirty-five Years

Transportation			5.2% -	6.2%
• Gasoline and motor oil	3.6% - 4.3%			
• Public transportation	0.7% - 0.8%			
• Vehicle maintenance and repairs	1.0% - 1.2%			
Food			9.5% -	10.0%
• Food at home	5.6% - 5.6%			
• Food away from home	3.9% - 4.4%			
Health care			1.4% -	1.4%
• Medical services	1.0% - 1.0%			
• Drugs	0.4% - 0.4%			
• Medical supplies	0.1% - 0.1%			
Other			2.4% -	2.7%
• Alcoholic beverages	0.4% - 0.7%			
• Personal care products and services	0.8% - 0.9%			
• Reading	0.1% - 0.1%			
• Education	1.1% - 1.1%			
DISCRETIONARY OBLIGATIONS			**7.8% -**	**9.3%**
Apparel and Services			3.0% -	3.4%
• Men and boys	0.7% - 0.8%			
• Women and girls	1.1% - 1.2%			
• Children under 2	0.3% - 0.4%			
• Footwear	0.6% - 0.6%			
• Other apparel products and services	0.3% - 0.4%			
Entertainment			2.5% -	3.4%
• Fees and admissions	0.8% - 0.8%			
• Audio and visual equipment and services	0.9% - 1.4%			
• Pets, toys, hobbies, and playground equipment	0.4% - 0.6%			
• Other entertainment supplies, equipment, and services	0.4% - 0.6%			
Tobacco			0.0% -	0.0%
• Tobacco products and smoking supplies	0.0% - 0.0%			
Other			2.3% -	2.5%
• Cash contributions	1.8% - 1.8%			
• Miscellaneous	0.5% - 0.7%			
NET INCOME			**23.8% -**	**17.0%**

Table 7-1   Consumer unit income and obligation target ranges expressed as a percentage of gross income.

Head Between Thirty-five to Forty-four Years

CONSUMER INCOME STATEMENT TARGET RANGES Head Thirty-five to Forty-four Years						
GROSS INCOME				100.0%	-	100.0%
Wages and salaries	91.3%	-	91.3%			
Self-employment income	4.6%	-	4.6%			
Social Security, private and government retirement	1.2%	-	1.2%			
Interest, dividends, rental income, other property income	1.0%	-	1.0%			
Unemployment and workers' compensation, veterans' benefits	0.3%	-	0.3%			
Public assistance, supplemental security income, food stamps	0.6%	-	0.6%			
Regular contributions for support	0.8%	-	0.8%			
Other income	0.3%	-	0.3%			
PERSONAL TAXES				10.2%	-	10.2%
Federal income taxes	2.3%	-	2.3%			
State and local income taxes	0.7%	-	0.7%			
FICA	7.0%	-	7.0%			
Other taxes	0.2%	-	0.2%			
Investment Income Reinvestment				-1.0%	-	0.0%
DISPOSABLE INCOME				88.8%	-	89.8%
FIXED OBLIGATIONS				24.7%	-	26.5%
Housing				15.0%	-	15.8%
• Shelter	15.0%	-	15.8%			
Transportation				5.9%	-	6.9%
• Vehicles purchases	3.9%	-	4.6%			
• Vehicle finance charges	0.4%	-	0.4%			
• Vehicle insurance	1.1%	-	1.3%			
• Other vehicle expenses	0.5%	-	0.6%			
Health care				1.7%	-	1.7%
• Health insurance	1.7%	-	1.7%			
Other				2.1%	-	2.1%
• Life and other personal insurance	0.4%	-	0.4%			
• Pensions	1.8%	-	1.8%			
VARIABLE OBLIGATIONS				25.9%	-	28.8%
Housing				9.1%	-	10.6%
• Utilities, fuels, and public services	4.4%	-	5.1%			
• Household operations	1.7%	-	1.9%			
• Housekeeping supplies	0.8%	-	0.8%			
• Household furnishings and equipment	2.3%	-	2.7%			
Transportation				4.3%	-	5.1%
• Gasoline and motor oil	2.7%	-	3.1%			
• Public transportation	0.7%	-	0.8%			
• Vehicle maintenance and repairs	1.0%	-	1.2%			

CONSUMER INCOME STATEMENT TARGET RANGES
Head Thirty-five to Forty-four Years

Food				8.8% -	9.2%
• Food at home	5.4%	-	5.4%		
• Food away from home	3.4%	-	3.8%		
Health care				1.4% -	1.4%
• Medical services	0.9%	-	0.9%		
• Drugs	0.4%	-	0.4%		
• Medical supplies	0.1%	-	0.1%		
Other				2.3% -	2.3%
• Alcoholic beverages	0.3%	-	0.3%		
• Personal care products and services	0.8%	-	0.8%		
• Reading	0.1%	-	0.1%		
• Education	1.1%	-	1.1%		
DISCRETIONARY OBLIGATIONS				**7.9% -**	**9.3%**
Apparel and Services				2.5% -	2.8%
• Men and boys	0.6%	-	0.7%		
• Women and girls	0.9%	-	1.1%		
• Children under 2	0.1%	-	0.2%		
• Footwear	0.4%	-	0.5%		
• Other apparel products and services	0.3%	-	0.4%		
Entertainment				2.8% -	3.7%
• Fees and admissions	1.1%	-	1.2%		
• Audio and visual equipment and services	0.8%	-	1.2%		
• Pets, toys, hobbies, and playground equipment	0.5%	-	0.7%		
• Other entertainment supplies, equipment, and services	0.4%	-	0.6%		
Tobacco				0.0% -	0.0%
• Tobacco products and smoking supplies	0.0%	-	0.0%		
Other				2.6% -	2.8%
• Cash contributions	2.0%	-	2.0%		
• Miscellaneous	0.6%	-	0.8%		
NET INCOME				**30.3% -**	**25.1%**

Table 7-2   Consumer unit income and obligation target ranges expressed as a percentage of gross income.

155

Head Between Forty-five and Fifty-four Years

CONSUMER INCOME STATEMENT TARGET RANGES					
Head Forty-five to Fifty-four Years					
GROSS INCOME			**100.0%**	**-**	**100.0%**
Wages and salaries	86.9%	- 86.9%			
Self-employment income	6.6%	- 6.6%			
Social Security, private and government retirement	2.9%	- 2.9%			
Interest, dividends, rental income, other property income	1.8%	- 1.8%			
Unemployment and workers' compensation, veterans' benefits	0.4%	- 0.4%			
Public assistance, supplemental security income, food stamps	0.4%	- 0.4%			
Regular contributions for support	0.7%	- 0.7%			
Other income	0.2%	- 0.2%			
PERSONAL TAXES			**11.0%**	**-**	**11.0%**
Federal income taxes	3.1%	- 3.1%			
State and local income taxes	0.9%	- 0.9%			
FICA	6.6%	- 6.6%			
Other taxes	0.3%	- 0.3%			
Investment income reinvestment			-1.8%	-	0.0%
DISPOSABLE INCOME			**87.2%**	**-**	**89.0%**
FIXED OBLIGATIONS			**21.5%**	**-**	**23.0%**
Housing			12.3%	-	13.0%
• Shelter	12.3%	- 13.0%			
Transportation			4.9%	-	5.7%
• Vehicles purchases	2.9%	- 3.3%			
• Vehicle finance charges	0.3%	- 0.3%			
• Vehicle insurance	1.2%	- 1.4%			
• Other vehicle expenses	0.5%	- 0.6%			
Health care			1.7%	-	1.7%
• Health insurance	1.7%	- 1.7%			
Other			2.6%	-	2.6%
• Life and other personal insurance	0.5%	- 0.5%			
• Pensions	2.1%	- 2.1%			
VARIABLE OBLIGATIONS			**25.2%**	**-**	**27.9%**
Housing			7.6%	-	8.9%
• Utilities, fuels, and public services	4.0%	- 4.8%			
• Household operations	1.0%	- 1.1%			
• Housekeeping supplies	0.8%	- 0.9%			
• Household furnishings and equipment	1.8%	- 2.2%			
Transportation			4.4%	-	5.1%
• Gasoline and motor oil	2.5%	- 2.9%			
• Public transportation	0.8%	- 0.9%			
• Vehicle maintenance and repairs	1.1%	- 1.3%			

CONSUMER INCOME STATEMENT TARGET RANGES
Head Forty-five to Fifty-four Years

Food		8.1% -	8.5%
• Food at home	5.0% - 5.0%		
• Food away from home	3.2% - 3.6%		
Health care		1.7% -	1.7%
• Medical services	1.0% - 1.0%		
• Drugs	0.6% - 0.6%		
• Medical supplies	0.2% - 0.2%		
Other		3.3% -	3.6%
• Alcoholic beverages	0.3% - 0.5%		
• Personal care products and services	0.8% - 0.9%		
• Reading	0.2% - 0.2%		
• Education	2.1% - 2.1%		
DISCRETIONARY OBLIGATIONS		**7.6% -**	**9.0%**
Apparel and Services		2.2% -	2.5%
• Men and boys	0.5% - 0.6%		
• Women and girls	1.0% - 1.1%		
• Children under 2	0.1% - 0.1%		
• Footwear	0.4% - 0.4%		
• Other apparel products and services	0.2% - 0.3%		
Entertainment		2.4% -	3.1%
• Fees and admissions	0.9% - 1.0%		
• Audio and visual equipment and services	0.7% - 1.0%		
• Pets, toys, hobbies, and playground equipment	0.4% - 0.7%		
• Other entertainment supplies, equipment, and services	0.3% - 0.5%		
Tobacco		0.0% -	0.0%
• Tobacco products and smoking supplies	0.0% - 0.0%		
Other		3.1% -	3.3%
• Cash contributions	2.4% - 2.4%		
• Miscellaneous	0.6% - 0.9%		
NET INCOME		**32.9% -**	**29.1%**

Table 7-3 Consumer unit income and obligation target ranges expressed as a percentage of gross income.

Head Between Fifty-five and Sixty-four Years

CONSUMER INCOME STATEMENT TARGET RANGES Head Fifty-five to Sixty-four Years					
GROSS INCOME			**100.0%**	**-**	**100.0%**
Wages and salaries	76.0%	- 76.0%			
Self-employment income	6.3%	- 6.3%			
Social Security, private and government retirement	12.3%	- 12.3%			
Interest, dividends, rental income, other property income	3.7%	- 3.7%			
Unemployment and workers' compensation, veterans' benefits	0.4%	- 0.4%			
Public assistance, supplemental security income, food stamps	0.5%	- 0.5%			
Regular contributions for support	0.7%	- 0.7%			
Other income	0.2%	- 0.2%			
PERSONAL TAXES			**10.2%**	**-**	**10.2%**
Federal income taxes	3.1%	- 3.1%			
State and local income taxes	0.8%	- 0.8%			
FICA	5.8%	- 5.8%			
Other taxes	0.4%	- 0.4%			
Investment income reinvestment			-3.7%	-	0.0
DISPOSABLE INCOME			**86.1%**	**-**	**89.3%**
FIXED OBLIGATIONS			**21.8%**	**-**	**23.4%**
Housing			11.0%	-	11.7%
• Shelter	11.0%	- 11.7%			
Transportation			5.5%	-	6.4%
• Vehicles purchases	3.4%	- 3.9%			
• Vehicle finance charges	0.3%	- 0.4%			
• Vehicle insurance	1.2%	- 1.4%			
• Other vehicle expenses	0.6%	- 0.7%			
Health care			2.5%	-	2.5%
• Health insurance	2.5%	- 2.5%			
Other			2.9%	-	2.9%
• Life and other personal insurance	0.6%	- 0.6%			
• Pensions	2.3%	- 2.3%			
VARIABLE OBLIGATIONS			**26.2%**	**-**	**29.0%**
Housing			8.4%	-	9.7%
• Utilities, fuels, and public services	4.0%	- 4.8%			
• Household operations	1.1%	- 1.2%			
• Housekeeping supplies	1.1%	- 1.3%			
• Household furnishings and equipment	2.2%	- 2.5%			
Transportation			4.7%	-	5.5%
• Gasoline and motor oil	2.5%	- 2.9%			
• Public transportation	1.1%	- 1.2%			
• Vehicle maintenance and repairs	1.1%	- 1.4%			

CONSUMER INCOME STATEMENT TARGET RANGES
Head Fifty-five to Sixty-four Years

Food			8.0% -	8.4%
• Food at home	4.9% -	4.9%		
• Food away from home	3.1% -	3.5%		
Health care			2.4% -	2.4%
• Medical services	1.2% -	1.2%		
• Drugs	0.9% -	0.9%		
• Medical supplies	0.2% -	0.2%		
Other			2.7% -	3.0%
• Alcoholic beverages	0.4% -	0.6%		
• Personal care products and services	0.8% -	0.9%		
• Reading	0.2% -	0.2%		
• Education	1.3% -	1.3%		
DISCRETIONARY OBLIGATIONS			**9.1% -**	**10.4%**
Apparel and Services			2.1% -	2.4%
• Men and boys	0.4% -	0.5%		
• Women and girls	0.9% -	1.1%		
• Children under 2	0.1% -	0.1%		
• Footwear	0.4% -	0.4%		
• Other apparel products and services	0.3% -	0.3%		
Entertainment			2.3% -	3.1%
• Fees and admissions	0.8% -	0.9%		
• Audio and visual equipment and services	0.7% -	1.0%		
• Pets, toys, hobbies, and playground equipment	0.5% -	0.7%		
• Other entertainment supplies, equipment, and services	0.3% -	0.5%		
Tobacco			0.0% -	0.0%
• Tobacco products and smoking supplies	0.0% -	0.0%		
Other			4.6% -	4.9%
• Cash contributions	3.9% -	3.9%		
• Miscellaneous	0.8% -	1.1%		
NET INCOME			**29.0% -**	**27.0%**

Table 7-4   Consumer unit income and obligation target ranges expressed as a percentage of gross income.

Head Between Sixty-five to Seventy-four Years

CONSUMER INCOME STATEMENT TARGET RANGES					
Head Sixty-five to Seventy-four Years					
GROSS INCOME			**100.0%**	**-**	**100.0%**
Wages and salaries	38.8%	- 38.8%			
Self-employment income	6.0%	- 6.0%			
Social Security, private and government retirement	47.4%	- 47.4%			
Interest, dividends, rental income, other property income	6.4%	- 6.4%			
Unemployment and workers' compensation, veterans' benefits	0.2%	- 0.2%			
Public assistance, supplemental security income, food stamps	0.6%	- 0.6%			
Regular contributions for support	0.3%	- 0.3%			
Other income	0.3%	- 0.3%			
PERSONAL TAXES	5.8%	5.8%	**5.8%**	**-**	**5.8%**
Federal income taxes	2.1%	- 2.1%			
State and local income taxes	0.3%	- 0.3%			
FICA	3.0%	- 3.0%			
Other taxes	0.5%	- 0.5%			
Investment income reinvestment			0.0%	-	0.0%
DISPOSABLE INCOME			**94.2%**	**-**	**94.2%**
FIXED OBLIGATIONS			**25.4%**	**-**	**27.4%**
Housing			11.4%	-	12.2%
• Shelter	11.4%	- 12.2%			
Transportation			6.0%	-	6.8%
• Vehicles purchases	3.5%	- 4.0%			
• Vehicle finance charges	0.3%	- 0.3%			
• Vehicle insurance	1.7%	- 2.0%			
• Other vehicle expenses	0.4%	- 0.5%			
Health care		5.9%	5.9%	-	5.9%
• Health insurance	5.9%	- 5.9%			
Other			2.1%	-	2.5%
• Life and other personal insurance	0.8%	- 0.8%			
• Pensions	1.3%	- 1.7%			
VARIABLE OBLIGATIONS			**31.3%**	**-**	**35.6%**
Housing			10.3%	-	13.2%
• Utilities, fuels, and public services	5.3%	- 7.1%			
• Household operations	1.3%	- 1.5%			
• Housekeeping supplies	1.2%	- 1.4%			
• Household furnishings and equipment	2.4%	- 3.2%			
Transportation			4.6%	-	5.4%
• Gasoline and motor oil	2.4%	- 2.8%			
• Public transportation	0.9%	- 1.0%			
• Vehicle maintenance and repairs	1.3%	- 1.6%			

CONSUMER INCOME STATEMENT TARGET RANGES
Head Sixty-five to Seventy-four Years

Food				10.2%	-	10.6%
• Food at home	7.0%	-	7.0%			
• Food away from home	3.1%	-	3.5%			
Health care				3.9%	-	3.9%
• Medical services	1.8%	-	1.8%			
• Drugs	1.8%	-	1.8%			
• Medical supplies	0.3%	-	0.3%			
Other				2.3%	-	2.6%
• Alcoholic beverages	0.4%	-	0.5%			
• Personal care products and services	1.1%	-	1.3%			
• Reading	0.3%	-	0.3%			
• Education	0.5%	-	0.5%			
DISCRETIONARY OBLIGATIONS				**9.5%**	**-**	**11.0%**
Apparel and Services				2.2%	-	2.5%
• Men and boys	0.4%	-	0.5%			
• Women and girls	1.1%	-	1.3%			
• Children under 2	0.1%	-	0.1%			
• Footwear	0.4%	-	0.4%			
• Other apparel products and services	0.3%	-	0.3%			
Entertainment				2.4%	-	3.3%
• Fees and admissions	0.8%	-	0.9%			
• Audio and visual equipment and services	0.7%	-	1.1%			
• Pets, toys, hobbies, and playground equipment	0.4%	-	0.5%			
• Other entertainment supplies, equipment, and services	0.5%	-	0.8%			
Tobacco				0.0%	-	0.0%
• Tobacco products and smoking supplies	0.0%	-	0.0%			
Other				4.9%	-	5.2%
• Cash contributions	4.0%	-	4.0%			
• Miscellaneous	0.8%	-	1.2%			
NET INCOME					**-**	

Table 7-5   Consumer unit income and obligation target ranges expressed as a percentage of gross income.

Head > Seventy-four Years

CONSUMER INCOME STATEMENT TARGET RANGES Head Over Seventy-four Years					
GROSS INCOME			**100.0%**	**-**	**100.0%**
Wages and salaries	15.9%	- 15.9%			
Self-employment income	3.3%	- 3.3%			
Social Security, private and government retirement	64.1%	- 64.1%			
Interest, dividends, rental income, other property income	14.6%	- 14.6%			
Unemployment and workers' compensation, veterans' benefits	0.9%	- 0.9%			
Public assistance, supplemental security income, food stamps	0.6%	- 0.6%			
Regular contributions for support	0.4%	- 0.4%			
Other income	0.2%	- 0.2%			
PERSONAL TAXES			**3.9%**	**-**	**3.9%**
Federal income taxes	1.6%	- 1.6%			
State and local income taxes	0.5%	- 0.5%			
FICA	1.2%	- 1.2%			
Other taxes	0.7%	- 0.7%			
Investment income reinvestment			0.0%	-	0.0%
DISPOSABLE INCOME			**96.1%**	**-**	**96.1%**
FIXED OBLIGATIONS			**18.1%**	**-**	**23.6%**
Housing			4.6%	-	9.2%
• Shelter	4.6%	- 9.2%			
Transportation			4.0%	-	4.6%
• Vehicles purchases	2.3%	- 2.7%			
• Vehicle finance charges	0.1%	- 0.1%			
• Vehicle insurance	1.1%	- 1.3%			
• Other vehicle expenses	0.5%	- 0.5%			
Health care			8.4%	-	8.4%
• Health insurance	8.4%	- 8.4%			
Other			1.1%	-	1.4%
• Life and other personal insurance	0.9%	- 0.9%			
• Pensions	0.2%	- 0.5%			
VARIABLE OBLIGATIONS			**37.0%**	**-**	**41.7%**
Housing			11.8%	-	15.2%
• Utilities, fuels, and public services	6.5%	- 8.7%			
• Household operations	2.6%	- 2.9%			
• Housekeeping supplies	1.3%	- 1.4%			
• Household furnishings and equipment	1.5%	- 2.2%			
Transportation			4.8%	-	5.5%
• Gasoline and motor oil	2.0%	- 2.3%			
• Public transportation	1.8%	- 1.9%			
• Vehicle maintenance and repairs	1.1%	- 1.3%			

CONSUMER INCOME STATEMENT TARGET RANGES Head Over Seventy-four Years				
Food			10.7% -	11.1%
• Food at home	7.4%	- 7.4%		
• Food away from home	3.2%	- 3.7%		
Health care			6.6% -	6.6%
• Medical services	3.2%	- 3.2%		
• Drugs	2.9%	- 2.9%		
• Medical supplies	0.6%	- 0.6%		
Other			3.1% -	3.4%
• Alcoholic beverages	0.3%	- 0.5%		
• Personal care products and services	1.2%	- 1.4%		
• Reading	0.4%	- 0.4%		
• Education	1.0%	- 1.0%		
DISCRETIONARY OBLIGATIONS			**15.6% -**	**17.9%**
Apparel and Services			1.8% -	2.1%
• Men and boys	0.4%	- 0.4%		
• Women and girls	0.9%	- 1.0%		
• Children under 2	0.0%	- 0.0%		
• Footwear	0.3%	- 0.3%		
• Other apparel products and services	0.3%	- 0.3%		
Entertainment			4.8% -	6.4%
• Fees and admissions	1.6%	- 1.7%		
• Audio and visual equipment and services	1.2%	- 1.9%		
• Pets, toys, hobbies, and playground equipment	0.7%	- 1.0%		
• Other entertainment supplies, equipment, and services	1.3%	- 1.9%		
Tobacco			0.0% -	0.0%
• Tobacco products and smoking supplies	0.0%	- 0.0%		
Other			9.0% -	9.4%
• Cash contributions	8.2%	- 8.2%		
• Miscellaneous	0.8%	- 1.2%		
NET INCOME			**25.4% -**	**12.9%**

Table 7-6   Consumer unit income and obligation target ranges expressed as a percentage of gross income.

Consumer Statements of Financial Condition

Head Under Thrity-five Years

CONSUMER STATEMENT OF FINANCIAL CONDITION Head Under Thirty-five Years					
ASSETS			**318.9%**	**-**	**489.4%**
CURRENT ASSETS			19.2%	-	57.5%
Cash			16.7%	-	20.8%
Short-Term Investments			2.5%	-	36.7%
LONG-TERM ASSETS			299.7%	-	431.9%
Financial Assets			27.0%	-	29.9%
• Bonds	2.1%	- 2.5%			
• Stocks	14.3%	- 16.9%			
• Pooled Investment Funds	6.1%	- 6.1%			
• Cash-Value Life Insurance	3.0%	- 3.0%			
• Other Managed Assets	0.4%	- 0.4%			
• Other Financial Assets	1.1%	- 1.1%			
Retirement Accounts			7.5%	-	115.0%
Nonfinancial Assets			265.2%	-	286.9%
• Primary Residence	157.5%	- 165.8%			
• Other Residential Real Estate	15.0%	- 16.5%			
• Owned Vehicles	21.8%	- 26.1%			
• Net Equity in Nonresidential Real Estate	7.3%	- 8.1%			
• Business Equity	61.0%	- 67.5%			
• Other Nonfinancial Assets	2.6%	- 2.9%			
FINANCIAL OBLIGATIONS			**200.7%**	**-**	**219.1%**
CURRENT OBLIGATIONS			65.8%	-	73.3%
Fixed Obligations			28.5%	-	30.9%
• Housing	17.5%	- 18.4%			
Shelter	*17.5%*	*- 18.4%*			
• Transportation	7.4%	- 8.9%			
Vehicles Purchases	*5.7%*	*- 6.9%*			
Vehicle Insurance	*1.2%*	*- 1.4%*			
Vehicle Finance Charges	*0.6%*	*- 0.7%*			
• Health Care	1.6%	- 1.6%			
Health Insurance	*1.6%*	*- 1.6%*			
• Other	1.9%	- 1.9%			
Life and Other Personal Insurance	*0.3%*	*- 0.3%*			
Pensions	*1.7%*	*- 1.7%*			

CONSUMER STATEMENT OF FINANCIAL CONDITION
Head Under Thirty-five Years

					31.9%		35.6%
Variable Obligations							
• **Housing**	10.2%	-	**11.9%**				
Utilities	4.5%	-	5.3%				
Operations	3.0%	-	3.6%				
Supplies	1.8%	-	2.1%				
Furnishings and Equipment	0.8%	-	0.9%				
• **Transportation**	5.9%	-	**7.1%**				
Gasoline and Motor Oil	3.6%	-	4.3%				
Vehicle Maintenance and Repairs	1.0%		1.2%				
Other Vehicle Expenses	0.7%	-	0.9%				
Public Transportation	0.7%	-	0.8%				
• **Food**	9.5%	-	**10.0%**				
At Home	5.6%	-	5.6%				
Away from Home	3.9%	-	4.4%				
• **Health care**	1.4%	-	**1.4%**				
Medical Services	1.0%	-	1.0%				
Drugs	0.4%	-	0.4%				
Medical Supplies	0.1%	-	0.1%				
• **Other**	4.7%	-	**5.3%**				
Alcoholic Beverages	0.4%	-	0.7%				
Personal Care Products and Services	0.8%	-	0.9%				
Reading	0.1%	-	0.1%				
Education	1.1%	-	1.1%				
Cash Contributions	1.8%	-	1.8%				
Miscellaneous	0.5%	-	0.7%				
Discretionary Obligations					5.5%	-	6.8%
• **Apparel and Services**	3.0%	-	**3.4%**				
Women and Girls	1.1%	-	1.2%				
Men and Boys	0.7%	-	0.8%				
Footwear	0.6%	-	0.6%				
Children under 2	0.3%	-	0.4%				
Other	0.3%	-	0.4%				
• **Entertainment**	2.5%	-	**3.4%**				
Audio/Visual Equipment and Services	0.9%	-	1.4%				
Fees and Admissions	0.8%	-	0.8%				
Pets, Toys, Hobbies, and Playground Equipment	0.4%	-	0.6%				
Other	0.4%	-	0.6%				
Frivolous Obligations					0.0%	-	0.0%
• **Tobacco**	0.0%	-	**0.0%**				

CONSUMER STATEMENT OF FINANCIAL CONDITION Head Under Thirty-five Years					
LONG-TERM OBLIGATIONS			**134.9%**	**-**	**145.8%**
• **Home-Secured Debt**	**109.6%**	**- 115.7%**			
Mortgages or Home Equity Loans	*100.3%*	*- 105.6%*			
Home Equity Lines of Credit	*2.6%*	*- 2.8%*			
Other Residential Real Estate Debt	*6.6%*	*- 7.3%*			
• **Installment Loans**	**22.7%**	**- 26.2%**			
Vehicle Loans	*9.0%*	*- 10.8%*			
Education Loans	*12.5%*	*- 13.9%*			
Other Installment Loans	*1.1%*	*- 1.4%*			
• **Credit Card Balances**	**2.2%**	**- 3.2%**			
• **Other Lines of Credit**	**0.1%**	**- 0.1%**			
• **Other Debt**	**0.4%**	**- 0.6%**			
NET WORTH			**118.2%**	**-**	**270.35%**

Table 7-7   Consumer assets and financial obligations as a percent of pretax income.

Head Thirty-five to Forty-four Years

CONSUMER STATEMENT OF FINANCIAL CONDITION Head Thirty-five to Forty-four Years					
ASSETS			**655.4%**	**-**	**935.2%**
CURRENT ASSETS			**41.7%**	**-**	**71.1%**
Cash			16.7%	-	20.8%
Short-Term Investments			25.0%	-	50.3%
LONG-TERM ASSETS			**613.7%**	**-**	**864.0%**
Financial Assets			59.6%	-	60.9%
• Bonds	5.0%	- 5.3%			
• Stocks	18.0%	- 19.0%			
• Pooled Investment Funds	21.2%	- 21.2%			
• Cash-Value Life Insurance	5.5%	- 5.5%			
• Other Managed Assets	3.6%	- 3.6%			
• Other Financial Assets	6.2%	- 6.2%			
Retirement Accounts			147.5%	-	402.5%
Nonfinancial Assets			406.6%	-	400.7%
• Primary Residence	223.8%	- 212.7%			
• Other Residential Real Estate	46.9%	- 49.3%			
• Owned Vehicles	18.0%	- 15.0%			
• Net Equity in Nonresidential Real Estate	12.0%	- 12.6%			
• Business Equity	103.7%	- 108.9%			
• Other Nonfinancial Assets	2.2%	- 2.3%			
FINANCIAL OBLIGATIONS			**202.6%**	**-**	**220.7%**
CURRENT OBLIGATIONS			**58.5%**	**-**	**64.6%**
Fixed Obligations			24.2%	-	25.9%
• Housing	15.0%	- 15.8%			
Shelter	*15.0%*	- *15.8%*			
• Transportation	5.4%	- 6.3%			
Vehicles Purchases	*3.9%*	- *4.6%*			
Vehicle Insurance	*1.1%*	- *1.3%*			
Vehicle Finance Charges	*0.4%*	- *0.4%*			
• Health Care	1.7%	- 1.7%			
Health Insurance	*1.7%*	- *1.7%*			
• Other	2.1%	- 2.1%			
Life and Other Personal Insurance	*0.4%*	- *0.4%*			
Pensions	*1.8%*	- *1.8%*			

CONSUMER STATEMENT OF FINANCIAL CONDITION
Head Thirty-five to Forty-four Years

Variable Obligations			**29.0%**	**-**	**32.2%**
• **Housing**	**9.1%**	**- 10.6%**			
Utilities	4.4%	- 5.1%			
Operations	2.3%	- 2.7%			
Supplies	1.7%	- 1.9%			
Furnishings and Equipment	0.8%	- 0.8%			
• **Transportation**	**4.9%**	**- 5.7%**			
Gasoline and Motor Oil	2.7%	- 3.1%			
Vehicle Maintenance and Repairs	1.0%	1.2%			
Other Vehicle Expenses	0.5%	- 0.6%			
Public Transportation	0.7%	- 0.8%			
• **Food**	**8.8%**	**- 9.2%**			
At Home	5.4%	- 5.4%			
Away from Home	3.4%	- 3.8%			
• **Health care**	**1.4%**	**- 1.4%**			
Medical Services	0.9%	- 0.9%			
Drugs	0.4%	- 0.4%			
Medical Supplies	0.1%	- 0.1%			
• **Other**	**4.9%**	**- 5.4%**			
Alcoholic Beverages	0.3%	- 0.5%			
Personal Care Products and Services	0.8%	- 0.9%			
Reading	0.1%	- 0.1%			
Education	1.1%	- 1.1%			
Cash Contributions	2.0%	- 2.0%			
Miscellaneous	0.6%	- 0.8%			
Discretionary Obligations			**5.3%**	**-**	**6.5%**
• **Apparel and Services**	**2.5%**	**- 2.8%**			
Women and Girls	0.9%	- 1.1%			
Men and Boys	0.6%	- 0.7%			
Footwear	0.4%	- 0.5%			
Children under 2	0.1%	- 0.2%			
Other	0.3%	- 0.4%			
• **Entertainment**	**2.8%**	**- 3.7%**			
Audio/Visual Equipment and Services	0.8%	- 1.2%			
Fees and Aadmissions	1.1%	- 1.2%			
Pets, Toys, Hobbies, and Playground Equipment	0.5%	- 0.7%			
Other	0.4%	- 0.6%			
Frivolous Obligations			**0.0%**	**-**	**0.0%**
• **Tobacco**	**0.0%**	**- 0.0%**			

CONSUMER STATEMENT OF FINANCIAL CONDITION Head Thirty-five to Forty-four Years					
LONG-TERM OBLIGATIONS				**144.1%** -	**156.1%**
• **Home-Secured Debt**	**131.3%**	-	**139.3%**		
Mortgages or Home Equity Loans	*111.8%*	-	*118.1%*		
Home Equity Lines of Credit	*3.5%*	-	*3.7%*		
Other Residential Real Estate Debt	*15.9%*	-	*17.6%*		
• **Installment Loans**	**11.1%**	-	**13.2%**		
Vehicle Loans	*6.2%*	-	*7.2%*		
Education Loans	*3.1%*	-	*3.6%*		
Other Installment Loans	*1.9%*	-	*2.4%*		
• **Credit Card Balances**	**1.3%**	-	**2.6%**		
• **Other Lines of Credit**	**0.1%**	-	**0.3%**		
• **Other Debt**	**0.3%**	-	**0.6%**		
NET WORTH				**452.8%** -	**714.5%**

Table 7-8   Consumer assets and financial obligations as a percent of pretax income.

Head Forty-five Fifty-four Years

CONSUMER STATEMENT OF FINANCIAL CONDITION Head Forty-five to Fifty-four Years					
ASSETS			**914.9%**	**-**	**2121.1%**
CURRENT ASSETS			41.7$	-	88.4%
Cash					
			16.7%	-	20.8%
Short-Term Investments			25.0%	-	67.6%
LONG-TERM ASSETS			873.2%	-	2032.7%
Financial Assets			101.1%	-	101.2%
• Bonds	8.1%	- 8.2%			
• Stocks	18.5%	- 18.6%			
• Pooled Investment Funds	42.9%	- 42.9%			
• Cash-Value Life Insurance	10.5%	- 10.5%			
• Other Managed Assets	15.8%	- 15.8%			
• Other Financial Assets	5.2%	- 5.2%			
Retirement Accounts			177.5%	-	1352.5%
Nonfinancial Assets			594.7%	-	579.0%
• Primary Residence	274.0%	- 246.6%			
• Other Residential Real Estate	62.6%	- 65.7%			
• Owned Vehicles	19.9%	- 16.6%			
• Net Equity in Nonresidential Real Estate	30.2%	- 31.7%			
• Business Equity	197.2%	- 207.0%			
• Other Nonfinancial Assets	10.8%	- 11.3%			
FINANCIAL OBLIGATIONS			**184.0%**	**-**	**201.2%**
CURRENT OBLIGATIONS			54.3%	-	59.9%
Fixed Obligations			21.0%	-	22.5%
• Housing	12.3%	- 13.0%			
Shelter	*12.3%*	*- 13.0%*			
• Transportation	4.4%	- 5.1%			
Vehicles Purchases	*2.9%*	*- 3.3%*			
Vehicle Insurance	*1.2%*	*- 1.4%*			
Vehicle Finance Charges	*0.3%*	*- 0.3%*			
• Health Care	1.7%	- 1.7%			
Health Insurance	*1.7%*	*- 1.7%*			
• Other	2.6%	- 2.6%			
Life and Other Personal Insurance	*0.5%*	*- 0.5%*			
Pensions	*2.1%*	*- 2.1%*			

CONSUMER STATEMENT OF FINANCIAL CONDITION Head Forty-five to Fifty-four Years						
Variable Obligations				**28.8%**	**-**	**31.8%**
• **Housing**	**7.6%**	**-**	**8.9%**			
Utilities	*4.0%*	*-*	*4.8%*			
Operations	*1.8%*	*-*	*2.2%*			
Supplies	*1.0%*	*-*	*1.1%*			
Furnishings and Equipment	*0.8%*	*-*	*0.9%*			
• **Transportation**	**4.9%**	**-**	**5.7%**			
Gasoline and Motor Oil	*2.5%*	*-*	*2.9%*			
Vehicle Maintenance and Repairs	*1.1%*		*1.3%*			
Other Vehicle Expenses	*0.5%*	*-*	*0.6%*			
Public Transportation	*0.8%*	*-*	*0.9%*			
• **Food**	**8.1%**	**-**	**8.5%**			
At Home	*5.0%*	*-*	*5.0%*			
Away from Home	*3.2%*	*-*	*3.6%*			
• **Health care**	**1.7%**	**-**	**1.7%**			
Medical Services	*1.0%*	*-*	*1.0%*			
Drugs	*0.6%*	*-*	*0.6%*			
Medical Supplies	*0.2%*	*-*	*0.2%*			
• **Other**	**6.4%**	**-**	**6.9%**			
Alcoholic Beverages	*0.3%*	*-*	*0.5%*			
Personal Care Products and Services	*0.8%*	*-*	*0.9%*			
Reading	*0.2%*	*-*	*0.2%*			
Education	*2.1%*	*-*	*2.1%*			
Cash Contributions	*2.4%*	*-*	*2.4%*			
Miscellaneous	*0.6%*	*-*	*0.9%*			
Discretionary Obligations				**4.6%**	**-**	**5.6%**
• **Apparel and Services**	**2.2%**	**-**	**2.5%**			
Women and Girls	*1.0%*	*-*	*1.1%*			
Men and Boys	*0.5%*	*-*	*0.6%*			
Footwear	*0.4%*	*-*	*0.4%*			
Children under 2	*0.1%*	*-*	*0.1%*			
Other	*0.2%*	*-*	*0.3%*			
• **Entertainment**	**2.4%**	**-**	**3.1%**			
Audio/visual Equipment and Services	*0.7%*	*-*	*1.0%*			
Fees and Admissions	*0.9%*	*-*	*1.0%*			
Pets, Toys, Hobbies, and Playground Equipment	*0.4%*	*-*	*0.7%*			
Other	*0.3%*	*-*	*0.5%*			
Frivolous Obligations				**0.0%**	**-**	**0.0%**
• **Tobacco**	**0.0%**	**-**	**0.0%**			

CONSUMER STATEMENT OF FINANCIAL CONDITION
Head Forty-five to Fifty-four Years

LONG-TERM OBLIGATIONS			129.6%	-	141.4%
• **Home-Secured Debt**	**119.7%**	- **127.4%**			
Mortgages or Home Equity Loans	*99.9%*	- *105.8%*			
Home Equity Lines of Credit	*5.4%*	- *5.8%*			
Other Residential Real Estate Debt	*14.3%*	- *15.9%*			
• **Installment Loans**	**10.0%**	- **12.1%**			
Vehicle Loans	*5.2%*	- *6.1%*			
Education Loans	*3.0%*	- *3.7%*			
Other Installment Loans	*1.7%*	- *2.3%*			
• **Credit Card Balances**	**0.0%**	- **1.4%**			
• **Other Lines of Credit**	**0.0%**	- **0.1%**			
• **Other Debt**	**0.0%**	- **0.4%**			
NET WORTH			**730.9%**	-	**1919.8%**

Table 7-9   Consumer assets and financial obligations as a percent of pretax income.

Head Fifty-five to Sixty-four Years

CONSUMER STATEMENT OF FINANCIAL CONDITION Head Fifty-five to Sixty-four Years					
ASSETS			**3259.6%**	**-**	**5310.6%**
CURRENT ASSETS			**41.7%**	**-**	**114.4%**
Cash			16.7%	-	20.8$
Short-Term Investments			25.0%	-	93.6%
LONG-TERM ASSETS			**3218.0%**	**-**	**5196.2%**
Financial Assets			**188.7%**	**-**	**190.5%**
• Bonds	8.6%	- 9.5%			
• Stocks	14.7%	- 15.7%			
• Pooled Investment Funds	107.4%	- 107.4%			
• Cash-Value Life Insurance	16.6%	- 16.6%			
• Other Managed Assets	30.6%	- 30.6%			
• Other Financial Assets	10.7%	- 10.7%			
Retirement Accounts			2230.0%	-	4230.0%
Nonfinancial Assets			799.3%	-	775.6%
• Primary Residence	291.9%	- 248.1%			
• Other Residential Real Estate	107.9%	- 113.3%			
• Owned Vehicles	24.2%	- 20.2%			
• Net Equity in Nonresidential Real Estate	65.1%	- 68.3%			
• Business Equity	300.1%	- 315.1%			
• Other Nonfinancial Assets	10.1%	- 10.6%			
FINANCIAL OBLIGATIONS			**172.1%**	**-**	**190.0%**
CURRENT OBLIGATIONS			**57.1%**	**-**	**62.9%**
Fixed Obligations			**21.3%**	**-**	**22.8%**
• Housing	11.0%	- 11.7%			
Shelter	_11.0%_	_- 11.7%_			
• Transportation	4.9%	- 5.7%			
Vehicles Purchases	_3.4%_	_- 3.9%_			
Vehicle Insurance	_1.2%_	_- 1.4%_			
Vehicle Finance Charges	_0.3%_	_- 0.4%_			
• Health Care	2.5%	- 2.5%			
Health Insurance	_2.5%_	_- 2.5%_			
• Other	2.9%	- 2.9%			
Life and Other Personal Insurance	_0.6%_	_- 0.6%_			
Pensions	_2.3%_	_- 2.3%_			

CONSUMER STATEMENT OF FINANCIAL CONDITION
Head Fifty-five to Sixty-four Years

Variable Obligations			**31.4%** -	**34.6%**
• **Housing**	**8.4%** -	**9.7%**		
Utilities	*4.0%* -	*4.8%*		
Operations	*2.2%* -	*2.5%*		
Supplies	*1.1%* -	*1.2%*		
Furnishings and Equipment	*1.1%* -	*1.3%*		
• **Transportation**	**5.3%** -	**6.2%**		
Gasoline and Motor Oil	*2.5%* -	*2.9%*		
Vehicle Maintenance and Repairs	*1.1%*	*1.4%*		
Other Vehicle Expenses	*0.6%* -	*0.7%*		
Public Transportation	*1.1%* -	*1.2%*		
• **Food**	**8.0%** -	**8.4%**		
At Home	*4.9%* -	*4.9%*		
Away from Home	*3.1%* -	*3.5%*		
• **Health Care**	**2.4%** -	**2.4%**		
Medical Services	*1.2%* -	*1.2%*		
Drugs	*0.9%* -	*0.9%*		
Medical Supplies	*0.2%* -	*0.2%*		
• **Other**	**7.3%** -	**7.9%**		
Alcoholic Beverages	*0.4%* -	*0.6%*		
Personal Care Products and Services	*0.8%* -	*0.9%*		
Reading	*0.2%* -	*0.2%*		
Education	*1.3%* -	*1.3%*		
Cash Contributions	*3.9%* -	*3.9%*		
Miscellaneous	**8.4%** -	*1.1%*		
Discretionary Obligations			**4.4%** -	**5.5%**
• **Apparel and Services**	**2.1%** -	**2.4%**		
Women and Girls	*0.9%* -	*1.1%*		
Men and Boys	*0.4%* -	*0.5%*		
Footwear	*0.4%* -	*0.4%*		
Children under 2	*0.1%* -	*0.1%*		
Other	*0.3%* -	*0.3%*		
• **Entertainment**	**2.3%** -	**3.1%**		
Audio/Visual Equipment and Services	*0.7%* -	*1.0%*		
Fees and Admissions	*0.8%* -	*0.9%*		
Pets, Toys, Hobbies, and Playground Equipment	*0.5%* -	*0.7%*		
Other	*0.3%* -	*0.5%*		
Frivolous Obligations			**0.0%** -	**0.0%**
• **Tobacco**	**0.0%** -	**0.0%**		

CONSUMER STATEMENT OF FINANCIAL CONDITION
Head Fifty-five to Sixty-four Years

LONG-TERM OBLIGATIONS			115.0%	-	127.2%
• *Home-Secured Debt*	*107.1%*	*- 114.7%*			
Mortgages or Home Equity Loans	79.2%	- 84.2%			
Home Equity Lines of Credit	6.0%	- 6.4%			
Other Residential Real Estate Debt	21.8%	- 24.1%			
• **Installment Loans**	**7.9%**	**- 10.2%**			
Vehicle Loans	5.0%	- 5.8%			
Education Loans	1.4%	- 2.1%			
Other Installment Loans	1.6%	- 2.4%			
• **Credit Card Balances**	**0.0%**	**- 1.5%**			
• **Other Lines of Credit**	**0.0%**	**- 0.1%**			
• **Other Debt**	**0.0%**	**- 0.6%**			
NET WORTH			**3087.5%**	**-**	**5120.6.%**

Table 7-10   Consumer assets and financial obligations as a percent of pretax income.

Head Sixty-five to Seventy-four Years

CONSUMER STATEMENT OF FINANCIAL CONDITION Head Sixty-five to Seventy-four Years					
ASSETS			**4008.8%**	**-**	**6249.3%**
CURRENT ASSETS			41.7%	-	118.0%
Cash			16.7%	-	20.8%
Short-Term Investments			25.0%	-	97.2%
LONG-TERM ASSETS			3967.2%	-	6131.2%
Financial Assets			295.5%	-	299.4%
• Bonds	13.2%	- 16.9%			
• Stocks	7.7%	- 7.9%			
• Pooled Investment Funds	154.1%	- 154.1%			
• Cash-Value Life Insurance	24.7%	- 24.7%			
• Other Managed Assets	75.9%	- 75.9%			
• Other Financial Assets	19.9%	- 19.9%			
Retirement Accounts			2507.5%	-	4735.0%
Nonfinancial Assets			1164.2%	-	1096.9%
• Primary Residence	462.5%	- 370.0%			
• Other Residential Real Estate	142.6%	- 149.8%			
• Owned Vehicles	29.6%	- 21.1%			
• Net Equity in Nonresidential Real Estate	95.7%	- 100.5%			
• Business Equity	409.1%	- 429.6%			
• Other Nonfinancial Assets	24.6%	- 25.9%			
FINANCIAL OBLIGATIONS			**169.7%**	**-**	**189.1%**
CURRENT OBLIGATIONS			66.2%	-	74.0%-
Fixed Obligations			24.9%	-	26.9%
• Housing	*11.4%*	- *12.2%*			
Shelter	*11.4%*	- *12.2%*			
• Transportation	**5.5%**	- **6.3%**			
Vehicles Purchases	*3.5%*	- *4.0%*			
Vehicle Insurance	*1.7%*	- *2.0%*			
Vehicle Finance Charges	*0.3%*	- *0.3%*			
• Health Care	**5.9%**	- **5.9%**			
Health Insurance	*5.9%*	- *5.9%*			
• Other	**2.1%**	- **2.5%**			
Life and Other Personal Insurance	*0.8%*	- *0.8%*			
Pensions	*1.3%*	- *1.7%*			

CONSUMER STATEMENT OF FINANCIAL CONDITION
Head Sixty-five to Seventy-four Years

Variable Obligations				36.6%	-	41.3%
• **Housing**	**10.3%**	**-**	**13.2%**			
Utilities	5.3%	-	7.1%			
Operations	2.4%	-	3.2%			
Supplies	1.3%	-	1.5%			
Furnishings and Equipment	1.2%	-	1.4%			
• **Transportation**	**5.1%**	**-**	**5.8%**			
Gasoline and Motor Oil	2.4%	-	2.8%			
Vehicle Maintenance and Repairs	1.3%		1.6%			
Other Vehicle Expenses	0.4%	-	0.5%			
Public Transportation	0.9%	-	1.0%			
• **Food**	**10.2%**	**-**	**10.6%**			
At Home	7.0%	-	7.0%			
Away from Home	3.1%	-	3.5%			
• **Health Care**	**3.9%**	**-**	**3.9%**			
Medical Services	1.8%	-	1.8%			
Drugs	1.8%	-	1.8%			
Medical Supplies	0.3%	-	0.3%			
• **Other**	**7.2%**	**-**	**7.8%**			
Alcoholic Beverages	0.4%	-	0.5%			
Personal Care Products and Services	1.1%	-	1.3%			
Reading	0.3%	-	0.3%			
Education	0.5%	-	0.5%			
Cash Contributions	4.0%	-	4.0%			
Miscellaneous	0.8%	-	1.2%			
Discretionary Obligations				4.7%	-	5.8%
• **Apparel and Services**	**2.2%**	**-**	**2.5%**			
Women and Girls	1.1%	-	1.3%			
Men and Boys	0.4%	-	0.5%			
Footwear	0.4%	-	0.4%			
Children under 2	0.1%	-	0.1%			
Other	0.3%	-	0.3%			
• **Entertainment**	**2.4%**	**-**	**3.3%**			
Audio/Visual Equipment and Services	0.7%	-	1.1%			
Fees and Admissions	0.8%	-	0.9%			
Pets, Toys, Hobbies, and Playground Equipment	0.4%	-	0.5%			
Other	0.5%	-	0.8%			
Frivolous Obligations				0.0%	-	0.0%
• **Tobacco**	**0.0%**	**-**	**0.0%**			

CONSUMER STATEMENT OF FINANCIAL CONDITION
Head Sixty-five to Seventy-four Years

LONG-TERM OBLIGATIONS			103.5%	-	115.1%
• **Home-Secured Debt**	**99.4%**	**-**	**106.8%**		
Mortgages or Home Equity Loans	74.5%	-	79.5%		
Home Equity Lines of Credit	4.5%	-	4.8%		
Other Residential Real Estate Debt	20.4%	-	22.5%		
• **Installment Loans**	**4.2%**	**-**	**5.4%**		
Vehicle Loans	4.2%	-	4.8%		
Education Loans	0.0%	-	0.2%		
Other Installment Loans	0.0%	-	0.4%		
• **Credit Card Balances**	**0.0%**	**-**	**1.6%**		
• **Other Lines of Credit**	**0.0%**	**-**	**0.7%**		
• **Other Debt**	**0.0%**	**-**	**0.6%**		
NET WORTH			**3839.1%**	**-**	**6060.1%**

Table 7-11   Consumer assets and financial obligations as a percent of pretax income.

Head >Seventy-four years

<table>
<tr><td colspan="6">CONSUMER STATEMENT OF FINANCIAL CONDITION
Head Over Seventy-four Years</td></tr>
<tr><td colspan="3">ASSETS</td><td>3816.4%</td><td>-</td><td>6048.9%</td></tr>
<tr><td colspan="3">CURRENT ASSETS</td><td>41.7%</td><td>-</td><td>118.0%</td></tr>
<tr><td colspan="3">Cash</td><td>16.7%</td><td>-</td><td>20.8%</td></tr>
<tr><td colspan="3">Short-Term Investments</td><td>25.0%</td><td>-</td><td>97.2%</td></tr>
<tr><td colspan="3">LONG-TERM ASSETS</td><td>3774.7%</td><td>-</td><td>5930.9%</td></tr>
<tr><td colspan="3">Financial Assets</td><td>267.1%</td><td>-</td><td>267.1%</td></tr>
<tr><td>• Bonds</td><td>1.1%</td><td>- 1.1%</td><td></td><td></td><td></td></tr>
<tr><td>• Stocks</td><td>10.3%</td><td>- 10.3%</td><td></td><td></td><td></td></tr>
<tr><td>• Pooled Investment Funds</td><td>102.8%</td><td>- 102.8%</td><td></td><td></td><td></td></tr>
<tr><td>• Cash-Value Life Insurance</td><td>28.6%</td><td>- 28.6%</td><td></td><td></td><td></td></tr>
<tr><td>• Other Managed Assets</td><td>110.6%</td><td>- 110.6%</td><td></td><td></td><td></td></tr>
<tr><td>• Other Financial Assets</td><td>13.7%</td><td>- 13.7%</td><td></td><td></td><td></td></tr>
<tr><td colspan="3">Retirement Accounts</td><td>2507.5%</td><td>-</td><td>4735.0%</td></tr>
<tr><td colspan="3">Nonfinancial Assets</td><td>1000.1%</td><td>-</td><td>928.8%</td></tr>
<tr><td>• Primary Residence</td><td>459.5%</td><td>- 367.6%</td><td></td><td></td><td></td></tr>
<tr><td>• Other Residential Real Estate</td><td>127.6%</td><td>- 134.0%</td><td></td><td></td><td></td></tr>
<tr><td>• Owned Vehicles</td><td>19.1%</td><td>- 13.7%</td><td></td><td></td><td></td></tr>
<tr><td>• Net Equity in Nonresidential Real Estate</td><td>99.7%</td><td>- 104.7%</td><td></td><td></td><td></td></tr>
<tr><td>• Business Equity</td><td>276.9%</td><td>- 290.8%</td><td></td><td></td><td></td></tr>
<tr><td>• Other Nonfinancial Assets</td><td>17.2%</td><td>- 18.1%</td><td></td><td></td><td></td></tr>
<tr><td colspan="3">FINANCIAL OBLIGATIONS</td><td>98.6%</td><td>-</td><td>114.9%</td></tr>
<tr><td colspan="3">CURRENT OBLIGATIONS</td><td>70.7%</td><td>-</td><td>83.2%</td></tr>
<tr><td colspan="3">Fixed Obligations</td><td>17.6%</td><td>-</td><td>23.0%</td></tr>
<tr><td>• Housing</td><td>4.6%</td><td>- 9.2%</td><td></td><td></td><td></td></tr>
<tr><td>Shelter</td><td>4.6%</td><td>- 9.2%</td><td></td><td></td><td></td></tr>
<tr><td>• Transportation</td><td>3.6%</td><td>- 4.1%</td><td></td><td></td><td></td></tr>
<tr><td>Vehicles Purchases</td><td>2.3%</td><td>- 2.7%</td><td></td><td></td><td></td></tr>
<tr><td>Vehicle Insurance</td><td>1.1%</td><td>- 1.3%</td><td></td><td></td><td></td></tr>
<tr><td>Vehicle Finance Charges</td><td>0.1%</td><td>- 0.1%</td><td></td><td></td><td></td></tr>
<tr><td>• Health Care</td><td>8.4%</td><td>- 8.4%</td><td></td><td></td><td></td></tr>
<tr><td>Health Insurance</td><td>8.4%</td><td>- 8.4%</td><td></td><td></td><td></td></tr>
<tr><td>• Other</td><td>1.1%</td><td>- 1.4%</td><td></td><td></td><td></td></tr>
<tr><td>Life and Other Personal Insurance</td><td>0.9%</td><td>- 0.9%</td><td></td><td></td><td></td></tr>
<tr><td>Pensions</td><td>0.2%</td><td>- 0.5%</td><td></td><td></td><td></td></tr>
</table>

CONSUMER STATEMENT OF FINANCIAL CONDITION Head Over Seventy-four Years					
Variable Obligations				**46.5%** -	**51.6%**
• **Housing**	**11.8%** -	**15.2%**			
Utilities	6.5% -	8.7%			
Operations	1.5% -	2.2%			
Supplies	2.6% -	2.9%			
Furnishings and Equipment	1.3% -	1.4%			
• **Transportation**	**5.3%** -	**6.1%**			
Gasoline and Motor Oil	2.0% -	2.3%			
Vehicle Maintenance and Repairs	1.1%	1.3%			
Other Vehicle Expenses	0.5% -	0.5%			
Public Transportation	1.8% -	1.9%			
• **Food**	**10.7%** -	**11.1%**			
At Home	7.4% -	7.4%			
Away from Home	3.2% -	3.7%			
• **Health care**	**6.6%** -	**6.6%**			
Medical Services	3.2% -	3.2%			
Drugs	2.9% -	2.9%			
Medical Supplies	0.6% -	0.6%			
• **Other**	**12.1%** -	**12.7%**			
Alcoholic Beverages	0.3% -	0.5%			
Personal Care Products and Services	1.2% -	1.4%			
Reading	0.4% -	0.4%			
Education	1.0% -	1.0%			
Cash Contributions	8.2% -	8.2%			
Miscellaneous	0.8% -	1.2%			
Discretionary Obligations				**6.6%** -	**8.5%**
• **Apparel and Services**	**1.8%** -	**2.1%**			
Women and Girls	0.9% -	1.0%			
Men and Boys	0.4% -	0.4%			
Footwear	0.3% -	0.3%			
Children under 2	0.0% -	0.0%			
Other	0.3% -	0.3%			
• **Entertainment**	**4.8%** -	**6.4%**			
Audio/Visual Equipment and Services	1.2% -	1.9%			
Fees and Admissions	1.6% -	1.7%			
Pets, Toys, Hobbies, and Playground Equipment	0.7% -	1.0%			
Other	1.3% -	1.9%			
Frivolous Obligations				**0.0%** -	**0.0%**
• **Tobacco**	**0.0%** -	**0.0%**			

CONSUMER STATEMENT OF FINANCIAL CONDITION
Head Over Seventy-four Years

LONG-TERM OBLIGATIONS					27.8%	-	31.8%
• **Home-Secured Debt**	**26.6%**	-	**28.5%**				
Mortgages or Home Equity Loans	*20.3%*	-	*21.7%*				
Home Equity Lines of Credit	*3.1%*	-	*3.3%*				
Other Residential Real Estate Debt	*3.2%*	-	*3.5%*				
• **Installment Loans**	**1.3%**	-	**1.5%**				
Vehicle Loans	*1.3%*	-	*1.4%*				
Education Loans	*0.0%*	-	*0.0%*				
Other Installment Loans	*0.0%*	-	*0.0%*				
• **Credit Card Balances**	**0.0%**	-	**0.6%**				
• **Other Lines of Credit**	**0.0%**	-	**0.3%**				
• **Other Debt**	**0.0%**	-	**0.9%**				
NET WORTH					**3717.8%**	**-**	**5934.0%**

Table 7-12   Consumer assets and financial obligations as a percent of pretax income.

INFORMATION SOURCES

- *Bureau of Labor Statistics.* <u>http://stats.bls.gov/cex/</u>/Consumer Expenditure Survey.
- *BusinessDictionary.com.* http://businessdictionary.com/
- Doniger, Marvin. 2009. *A Common Sense Approach to Successful Investing: Utilizing the Power of Stratamentical Analysis.* Bloomington IN: Xlibris Publishing.
- Doniger, Marvin. 2008. *A Common Sense Road Map to Uncommon Wealth: The Key to Financial Success.* Bloomington IN: iUniverse Inc.
- *Federal Reserve Board.* <u>http://www.federalreserve.gov/pubs/oss/oss2/scfindex.html/</u> Survey of Consumer Finances. *Federal Reserve Board.*http://www.federalreserve.gov/releases/housedebt/default.htm
- *Financial Times.* http://www.ft.com.
- *Investopedia.* http://www.investopedia.com/
- *Merriam-Webster Dictionary.* <u>http://www.merriam-webster.com/dictionary/quaestor</u>.
- *MSCI.* http://www.mscibarra.com.

GLOSSARY OF TERMS

Term	Meaning
Asset Allocation	A plan for maintaining a predetermined mix of investments in different types of assets.
Balance Sheet	A snapshot at a point in time of financial condition. It shows relationship between assets, obligations, and net worth.
CD **Certificate of Deposit**	A certificate issued by a bank that pays a fixed rate of interest for a term of one month to five years. Certificates of deposit are insured by the FDIC.
CDR **Consumer Debt Ratio**	The ratio of outstanding credit card and other consumer debt to disposable income.
Compound Returns	The returns generated from the reinvestment of earnings.
Consumer Unit	Members of a household.
Credit Card	Card used to buy products and services on credit.

Term	Meaning
Debt / Equity Ratio	An indication of the proportion of its financing comes from debt and equity. It is defined as the ratio of long-term debt to equity.
Debt / Income Ratio	An indication of how much gross monthly income goes toward monthly debt payment. It is the ratio of monthly debt to monthly gross income.
DSR **Debt Service Ratio**	The relationship between outstanding mortgage and consumer debt payments to disposable income.
Discretionary Obligations	Voluntary commitments.
Discretionary Obligations Coverage	Ratio of monthly gross income to the discretionary obligations due in the current month.
Disposable Income	The amount of income after taxes that is available for consumption and saving.
Diversification	Strategy for reducing risk by investing in different asset classes that do not move in same direction.
Equity Line of Credit	A line of credit secured by the equity in a specific property.
FDIC **Federal Deposit Insurance Corporation**	A federal agency one of whose responsibilities is to insure deposits up to $250,000.
FOR **Financial Obligation Ratio**	DSR plus automobile lease payments, rental payments on tenant occupied property, homeowners' insurance, and property tax payments.
Fixed Obligations	Periodic payments over a specific period of time.

Term	Meaning
Fixed Obligations Coverage	Ratio of monthly gross income to the fixed obligations due in the current month.
Gross Income	Income before taxes.
Housing Tenure	See Tenure.
Income Statement	A statement of sources of income and financial obligations over a specified period of time.
Income Surplus (Deficit)	Ratio of monthly gross income to the amount of income that remains after meeting that month's fixed, variable, and discretionary financial obligations.
Inflation	A trend of increasing prices for goods and services. Conversely, inflation is a depredation in purchasing power.
Laddering	Purchase of investment instruments with different maturities.
Leverage Ratio	Relationship between equity in assets to financial obligations.
Liquidity Ratio	A measure of the ability of a consumer unit to satisfy its current financial obligations with its current assets. It is the ratio of current assets to current liabilities.
Money Market Account	Interest bearing accounts from which checks can be written.
Mortgage	A loan used to finance purchase of real estate.
Net Income	Amount of money left after all financial obligations have been subtracted from gross income.

Term	Meaning
Net Worth	The difference between assets and liabilities.
Savings Bond	Debt securities issued by U.S. Treasury and backed by full faith and credit of U.S. government.
Tenure	Financial arrangements under which someone has the right to live in a home (home owner or renter).
Treasury Bills	Obligations of the U.S. Treasury that mature in less than one year.
Treasury Bonds	Obligations of the U.S. Treasury that mature in ten to thirty years.
Treasury Notes	Obligations of the U.S. Treasury that mature in two to ten years.
Variable Obligations	Obligations whose cost are based on the amount consumed.

INDEX

Edwards Brothers,Inc!
Thorofare, NJ 08086
13 April, 2011
BA2011103